"Time is always a premium commodity. Who ever has enough? With twenty years of experience in teaching women, my friend Cindi Ferrini can help maximize the time each of us is given. Rather than fret, why not focus on making the most of your days? Cindi can help you do that, and I highly recommend her seasoned wisdom on this topic."

—Barbara Rainey is a speaker, best-selling author, mother, grandmother, water color artist, and co-founder with husband Dennis of **Family**Life. They've co-authored numerous books including *Building Your Mates Self-Esteem* and *Moments with You*. Barbara's writings include *Thanksgiving: A Time to Remember* and *Barbara and Susan's Guide to the Empty Nest*.

"If you struggle to get organized, Cindi's *your new friend who understands*.

Rich Bible studies, practical tips, and thoughtful questions will enable you to develop a more balanced life. This is an ideal book to use in a women's study!"

—Susan Alexander Yates, speaker and author of a dozen books including, *And Then I Had Teenagers, Encouragement for Parents of Teens and Preteens* and *Barbara and Susan's Guide to the Empty Nest*.

I can hardly articulate all I want to say in one short paragraph. I thoroughly love the book and am putting it in our church's resource center, my gift to the women in my life. It's a must wedding gift, too. Thanks for the format and the topics. A lovely book!

—Karen Loritts - popular conference speaker, author, and teacher, married to Dr. Crawford Loritts for 39 years. They have served in full time ministry for 38 years - presently at Fellowship Bible Church in Roswell, GA. She is the mother of 4 married children and grandmother of 7.

This practical book gives us concrete ways to move ahead toward a balanced life. Cindi gives us questions to ask ourselves to help us achieve the lives we want—more peaceful, ordered lives. She has a heart to help us learn quickly what it has taken her years to discover.

—Joy Downs, speaker and co-author of *Fight Fair* and *One of Us Must Be Crazy and I'm Pretty Sure It's You!*

BALANCING
THE
ACTIVE LIFE

BALANCING THE ACTIVE LIFE

AN INTERACTIVE BIBLE STUDY

CINDI FERRINI

TATE PUBLISHING & Enterprises

Published by Tate Publishing & Enterprises, LLC
127 E. Trade Center Terrace | Mustang, Oklahoma 73064 USA
1.888.361.9473 | www.tatepublishing.com

Tate Publishing is committed to excellence in the publishing industry. The company reflects the philosophy established by the founders, based on Psalm 68:11,
"The Lord gave the word and great was the company of those who published it."

Book design copyright © 2011 by Tate Publishing, LLC. All rights reserved.
Cover design by April Marciszewski
Interior design by Lindsay B. Behrens

Published in the United States of America

ISBN: 978-1-61777-416-4
1. Religion / Christian Life / Inspirational
2. Religion / Christian Life / Personal Growth
11.08.17

ACKNOWLEDGEMENTS

Completing any project is a challenge. It takes a number of people, all juggling their talents, schedules, families, work, and emergencies, along with finding rest in the mix. Add to that mix the desire to live life in an orderly, godly, balanced way. It's not easy and must be intentional, and none of us are an exception; thus, it is with doses of reality that I share examples from our own family in this study, as well as thank those who contributed to it in the midst of their own busy lives:

- My husband Joe's encouragement and affirmation throughout this project has been as steady as he is. I appreciate having him at my side to share the joys, challenges, victories, and defeats as we continue learning to balance life together.

- The children (Joey, Kristina, and Kathleen) have always been my greatest teachers in the classroom of life. As our family increases with in-laws and grandchildren, the learning curve increases, as do the blessings. I am proud of who they have become and how they have learned to put balance into their own lives.

- Dr. Linda Meixner skillfully edited my initial document, graciously gave me consistent feedback as I requested it, and continues to teach me! Her influence reminds me that learning new things is exciting. Most importantly, she is a dear friend who cheers me on.

- Thank you to the team at Tate for their guidance, expertise, and excellence.

TABLE OF CONTENTS

INTRODUCTION

Balancing a pyramid of seven people on a tightrope cable only 5/8-inch thick, the Great Wallendas showed the world their astonishing skills. Over dens of lions, between buildings, and with no nets to catch them, they performed their balancing acts between thirty five and one hundred feet high. I wonder how this family dealt with the pressure. How many times did they nearly lose their balance? What was their secret to staying so calm and focused under *that* kind of pressure?

Who is to say that your life isn't just as stressful as you perform your own "acrobatic" and "balancing" act? What do you need to get through circumstances in life with the assurance and confidence of the Wallendas to cross confidently from one end of a tightrope to the other? (Of course you know not all the Wallendas made it safely...)

Some people don't think balance is possible; but examples of balance are all around us. Balance is defined as "bringing into harmony or proportion; to equalize in weight, numbers, or proportions; to bring or come to a state or position of balance." We want our checkbooks balanced at the end of the month. When we don't feel well, our bodies are not balanced and corrections need to be made—diet and exercise, or possibly medication and rest. We find balance in nature, science (chemistry, physics, biology), in music (harmony), in parenting (authoritative or permissive), and in our very own lives. We find ourselves overcommitted and under connected. When we are out of balance, we might show it with a poor attitude, frustration, anger, or feelings of being overwhelmed (stress). When our lives are balanced, we are peaceful, rested, kind, perhaps even generous. While checkbooks have a concreteness about being balanced, it is not so in all areas of our life, and so the balancing act begins.

When something in life challenges our balance (like a new baby, a job change, a move, a child with special needs, a death, a loss of friendship, too much work, not enough work, and you can add your own …), the key to balance is not having that balance in a locked position—like some state of perfection, but being able to move from side to side to accommodate the crisis or change. A balance wavers and fluctuates back and forth to accommodate the weights added to it, balancing between opposing forces. It's up to us to consider how God's wired us, how to make the proper adjustments in our own lives as to what our limits and limitations are, and to keep that balance as equalized as possible. It might be hiring a cleaning lady or lawn service for a time that is particularly busy, or realizing it's not affordable and opting to remove some activities that are really not within where we feel called. It's about our personal lives, not our neighbors'. It's not about being politically correct but correctly prioritized—without shame or embarrassment.

God's Word teaches us that he has it all under control: "A just balance and scales belong to the Lord; all the weights of the bag are his concern" (Proverbs 16:11). What God does for each of us, how he has gifted us, what he puts in our life, decisions he allows us to make, etc., are specifically for us, not someone else. Some of us will be able to handle more of some things, and others of us will not. God can help us live for today while we plan for the future. "Commit your works to the Lord, and your plans will be established" (Proverbs 16:3). And in those moments when we try to justify something we know God is telling us otherwise, he will examine our hearts. "Every man's way is right in his own eyes, but the Lord weighs the hearts" (Proverbs 21:2).

Do you want to balance the activities in your present schedule? Do you long for a simpler or fuller life? Will you choose to add what is lacking and delete or redefine what overwhelms? How willing are you to work at modifying the areas of your life that are out of control, out of balance? What are you willing to give up or add? Are you ready to recognize areas where you need to place limits—spending, friendships, work, or ... ? Are you willing to live differently, intentionally making choices, and choosing options that will fit your life? Balance is not about more, faster, bigger, better, or perfect, but God's best for us in our given situation. It's about learning to handle life one moment at a time in the present, yet looking to the future to what he has asked us to do. It's about considering the many good options we have before us and intentionally choosing the best. How does that look for you?

I hope that this study will help you balance your priorities, set and achieve goals, discipline and organize yourself in a variety of areas, and recognize that you can solve problem areas. You can do this thirteen week study alone or with your spouse, your family, or a small group. I believe any study works best when you do it with one or more other individuals who will hold you accountable to the goals you set while you hold them accountable to their goals.

Together we will evaluate the main areas needing balance and order in our lives today. You may wish to add others, because all of our lives are different. You may find that some areas need less fine-tuning than others. You and I don't have all the answers, but God does! As you realize that the Lord wants you to put balance and order into your life, you will enjoy the discipline and the excitement of having freedom in your schedule. Proverbs 11:1, "A false balance is an abomination to the Lord, but a just weight is His delight."

HOW TO USE THIS STUDY

Each lesson is intended to take sixty to ninety minutes to complete. Depending on the size of your group, you may want to break into smaller groups of three or four people so that the study can be completed in that length of time. It may also give everyone a chance to share answers, as well as suggestions. Alternating the facilitator can be a great way to allow others to lead in a very nonthreatening way. A facilitator doesn't have to "teach" or "preach." He or she just needs to keep things moving in an orderly fashion.

Let's Get Started begins each session. This section will lay a foundation for the topic to be discussed. Allow ten to fifteen minutes for each person to write her or his responses and for the group to discuss.

Today's Topic is a brief written study to read prior to the lesson, all participants on their own, then discuss it in a group. If you choose, it may be read aloud. Decide which works best for your group. Allow ten to fifteen minutes.

Stop, Look, and Listen gives your group a chance to stop and filter the information, look at what the Scriptures say, and listen to others. Sharing can be a vital part of this section. You'll get new ideas, learn that something worked for someone else, and then decide how to solve your own individual dilemmas. This section can be done ahead of time to allow more discussion. Allow thirty to forty minutes.

Next Step helps each person determine his or her next step. If we get too far ahead, things get foggy. We need to master one step at a time. Allow five to ten minutes.

Fine-Tuning will challenge each person to choose *one* action point to tackle the following week. Choosing more than one action point may cause frustration! Allow ten minutes.

On Your Own is to be done by an individual or by couples. It will challenge your thinking to form good habits. Take whatever time is needed on your own.

I have chosen not to write out each scripture verse. You must look them up on your own using the Bible translation of your choice. As you accept the challenge, I believe you will find many treasures!

SESSION ONE
WHERE DO I START?

Let's Get Started

1. On a day-to-day basis, what keeps you most busy?

   _____

2. Do you feel you live a balanced, well-ordered life? If
   yes, what do you do to maintain balance and order?
   If not, what do you feel is the greatest problem or
   frustration in falling short of achieving them?

   _____

3. Do you ever have moments/hours/days of boredom?
   Have you in the past?

   _____

I don't have time to be this busy!

Today's Topic

Psalm 90:9–10, 12 are some of my favorite verses. One day I decided to do something very practical. I decided to calculate how many days I would have to live if given the full seventy years mentioned in verse 10—or eighty if due to strength. It came to 25,550 days! At that time of my life, I averaged six hours of sleep each night, which amounted to 6,387 days. That left me with 19,161 days to live. My practical exercise forced me to draw some sobering conclusions. I can easily count to 19,161, so my life became shorter than I thought. And it becomes shorter for you and me when we subtract the number of days we've already lived! I suddenly understood the importance of each day, and came to realize that if we've wasted time, we might look back with regrets, sadness, and disappointment.

Those verses came alive to me as I evaluated the resources of time, energy, money, and talents the Lord has given me. I realized God created time and probably had something in mind to teach me about using it wisely for him. Those hopeful 19,161 days took on a new purpose for me. I became not only very time conscious but also more purposeful in the way I spent my time. Of the resources I just mentioned, the only one we all have in equal amounts on a daily basis is time. We are all given a twenty-four-hour day. What we do with each day is up to us and will reflect a lot about us.

How we spend our time *is* the life we live. We can learn to budget and gain discipline and control of our God-given resources, but if we are wasteful and overloaded or irresponsible, then we will deplete ourselves, leaving nothing in reserve.

Does being a Christian mean we automatically lead balanced lives? Hardly! Some don't believe we can work toward a "balanced" life. But because we have free choice in what we add or delete from our schedules, I think we do have the ability to work toward balance, it's whether we take the opportunity or not. In fact, as we sometimes get carried away with many good ministry opportunities, we may neglect the areas to which God is calling us, ones that are best for us. I hope, however, through this study, that you will discern the best ministry opportunities for you. Just as you must daily find time to go to work and care for your family, because doing so is a priority, you must also prioritize other areas to accomplish other things. You must make what God wants you to do a priority—a *top* priority because time passes quickly (Psalm 90:4).

In my own life, I have recognized times when things have gotten out of control—when I've allowed demanding or needy relationships to overtake my time and energy. Other times projects have piled up and that part of life seems out of control and unbalanced. Even early in our marriage, we began to see that we kept adding things to our life—our marriage, Bible studies, children, local and city ministry outreaches, and so on. There came a point when we stopped and recognized the need to evaluate which activities were most important and to which we felt particularly called.

We asked ourselves the following questions: How busy will I allow myself to be? How busy is busy enough? And who is the judge? Is what I'm involved in a passion, a calling, a way to fill my day? Will there be winners and losers in the busy game of life?

The hectic and hurried life out of balance is not only exhausting but also a puzzle. Why do we *allow* it? (And because we have choices, I do believe we *allow* it!) Some people seem overtaken by this way of life. Others don't like being swept into the hurried pace, and yet many continue driving in life's fast lane! Do we remain there because doing so allows us to avoid deeper issues, thoughts, and problems going on in our lives? Do we gain a sense of power and importance over others because we are so busy; or is God giving us the endurance, stamina, health, and calling—to keep going? These are puzzling questions we must answer for ourselves.

According to The Nielsen Wire online statistics, children watch some twenty-five hours of television per week; adults thirty-two to thirty-five hours a week, which comes to over five days a month—almost a full week! Add that to a seventy year life span, and we watch television more than 4,200 days! Imagine adding computer time. How can we be so bold to say "I'm too busy to do _____," or "I don't really have time," if we indeed spend that kind of time watching television? And if we indeed believe Scripture is true, there must be a *time for everything* because the Word says so in Ecclesiastes 3:1–8. I have learned that at certain times, we must put our fast-paced lives on hold. Emergencies, family illness, or death can *make* us stop! Suddenly, we have time we didn't think we had! During the original writing of this workbook, my father was hospitalized for nearly three months before coming home and needing full-time care. I was amazed at how much time I actually had to visit him and later help care for him at his home. When you *need* the time, you will find it. It might be turning off the television.

Is there a starting place? Is there a place to put priorities into place? We might start by trying to say the word *no.* Say it once out loud. Just remember that *saying "no" shouldn't be said in conjunction with how busy we are but according to our purposes, goals, responsibilities, and priorities*—the topics which we'll be studying in the next few sessions.

We can start by prioritizing what fills our lives. Some say we should prioritize in this order:

- Jesus
- Spouse
- Children
- Extended family
- Ministry/Church Activities
- Work
- Leisure

To simplify the above we can say, prioritize your life in this order: *Jesus, Others, Yourself.* This order will bring you *J.O.Y.* in living!

Others may say that our priorities should not be ordered lists, but we should instead put Christ at the center of everything, giving one hundred percent to each area God asks us to manage (Colossians1:18b).

Do we have to choose just one of the examples? Personally, I like them both! The question we must ask ourselves is this: How does God want *me* to prioritize each area? How does He want *me* to change so that I am at the center of His will?

Many will say, "Oh—that's okay for busy, young people, but you can't teach an old dog new tricks." Yet life changes all the time, we change all the time, and our spouses, friends, and children change all the time. (Read Psalm 107:33–38 to see what God can change and what the results are! And what can and will he do for you? Read 2 Corinthians 5:17.) We must individually accept the challenge to change—for the better—for God's best! If a balanced life is what we desire and we work toward it and achieve it, we must be prepared to handle comments from those who will judge us. Achieving a balanced life *does not* just happen. It *doesn't* occur by luck or chance but by working hard at what God has called each of us to do. *For a Christian, the balanced life is one that lines itself up according to biblical principles and priorities.* So let's get on with our study to learn to be all God wants us to be.

Stop—Look—Listen

1. Do you ever feel at "wit's end"? It's scriptural, you know! Read Psalm 107:23–31 and answer the following questions:

   vv. 25–26: What did the Lord do?

   _____

   _____

   _____

   v. 26a: How big were the waves?

   _____

   _____

   _____

   vv. 26b-27: What did the people feel?

   _____

   _____

   _____

vv. 28–29: Once they were at that point, what did they do? And how did the Lord respond?

_____

_____

_____

vv. 30–31: Then how did they feel?

_____

_____

_____

vv. 24–26: Look back. The people did not cause the storm. God did. What does that say to you about some of the things that come into your life? Is every situation that is beyond your control caused by you? Why do you think God *allowed* the storm to occur? When you are tossed about by life's storms and feel at wit's end, how do you *usually* respond?

_____

_____

_____

What *should* your response be?

_____

_____

_____

2. When you feel overloaded, overstressed, or too busy, and you feel as if you're reaching your "limit" (i.e., your breaking point), at what point do you stop?

_____

What makes you stop?

_____

_____

_____

3. Jesus lived a very active life. He had a lot of ministry to accomplish in three years. Although he was busy and active, he was not hurried. There was always more for Jesus to do. At what point did he stop and take a needed rest? Our Lord Jesus knew when to say "no"!

_____

Summarize the following verses:

- Matthew 4:1–11

_____

_____

- Mark 8:11–13

_____

_____

- Luke 4:38–44

_____

_____

- John 7:1–9

_____

_____

Start making time count!

Next Step

I've learned and often apply a principle for which I am thankful. When I believe I'm doing all God has asked of me, yet my life is bombarded with interruptions of all kinds, I realize I can't accomplish each task! I then ask the Lord to take the time available and multiply it as he multiplied the fish and loaves! (Read Matthew 14:16–21, 15:32–38; Mark 6:35–44; Luke 9:10–17; John 6:1–13.) I look at it this way: If God can multiply the fish and loaves, he can do it with time as well. I have experienced it! At times the clock just seems to stop (or at best, slows down!), sometimes I can't believe how much I can accomplish! It's a miraculous thing God can do! (Psalm 90:4; 2 Peter 3:8)

Do you need a new perspective on balancing your life?

Notice what he says about achieving balance as you read and summarize the following verses:

- Matthew 11:26–30

_____

_____

_____

- Proverbs 20:23

_____

_____

_____

- Proverbs 11:1

_____

_____

_____

1. Recognize the problem in lacking balance in your life. List *your* problem areas:

- _____

- _____

- _____

- _____

2. Realize you can solve some aspects of these problems and others, you can't. List both:

Problems I can solve if I choose to take action:

_____

_____ .

_____

_____

Problems I can't solve but will pray about:

_____

_____

_____

_____

3. Of the problems you can solve, list several actions you will take to solve them:

_____

_____

_____

_____

Fine-Tuning

Of the several actions you listed under **Next Step #3**, choose one and concentrate on it specifically this week:

- _____

On Your Own

Perhaps you've heard the phrase, *"Just do it!"* Can you? Can you stop saying some of the following phrases? (Then add your own frequent favorites!)

- "I'm too busy."
- "I don't have any free time."
- _____
- _____
- _____
- _____

How busy will you allow yourself to be?

_____

_____

_____

_____

How busy is busy enough?

_____

_____

_____

_____

Who's the judge?

_____

_____

_____

_____

Write out and memorize Psalm 90:12.

_____

_____

_____

_____

SESSION TWO
THE SECRET

Let's Get Started

List three areas in which you presently feel nonproductive in your use of time.

1. _____

2. _____

3. _____

What excuses do you make for your lack of productivity and unwise time management?

1. _____

2. _____

3. _____

4. _____

If you are serious about making the changes needed to balance your life, write down the name of someone who you believe would work with you and hold you accountable:

_____

Before you ask this individual, pray about it. Ask the Lord to provide a male (if you are a man); a gal (if you are a woman). Be sure to let her or him know that this commitment would end once this thirteen week study concludes. If you both should decide that continuing in this accountability relationship is advantageous, select another ending date. Continue reviewing until you're ready and able to be on your own, always setting a clear ending date. Most people are uncomfortable with an open-ended long-term commitment.

Today's Topic

I've heard it said that *May* is the best time for people who want to get busy and do things. "I *may* organize that closet. I *may* tune up that yard equipment. I *may* find the energy to start that project. I *may*…"

We all do it! We procrastinate. I have personally found that I procrastinate when the task is something I don't *really* want to start or do. I have a million excuses. And to me, they all sound great! But without a doubt, at some point excuses just don't hold much water, and I can no longer put off those tasks or projects that have by that time literally "gotten out of hand."

It reminds me of "The Grasshopper and the Ant" of Aesop's fables. The grasshopper was free spirited and fun loving. He happened to watch the ant struggling and sweating in the hot summer sun to move some food to his nesting area. After a while the grasshopper felt compelled to inquire about what the ant was up to. The ant replied that he was preparing for winter by gathering food and properly storing it. The grasshopper found that quite humorous and said to the ant, "It's such a beautiful day. Why don't you come with me and have some fun? You can do that later."

The ant refused, saying he had to prepare for winter, storing enough food to last until spring. The grasshopper continued to distract the ant, but to no avail.

Winter finally came. The grasshopper looked everywhere for food, but he found nothing. He was hungry and decided to go to the ant for some of his food. The ant replied, "You made the choice to play and have fun all summer while I worked and prepared for these cold winter months. Go play and have fun now. I will not give you a thing." And back to his cozy home the ant went.

The moral of the story is, "*Don't put off until tomorrow what you must do today.*"

Often when we procrastinate, we opt out of what God asks us to do, falling into the trap of expecting him to bail us out and get us back on track. Instead of doing that which is of importance, we can move only from crisis to crisis and feel as if we can never catch up to do what is most important.

None of us wants to be a procrastinator (Ecclesiastes 11:4–6), but like the grasshopper, it's sometimes more fun and easier to do *other* things instead of what we know we *should* be doing. We come up with excuses that sound pretty good to us, but making an excuse is usually how we show our disobedience to what God desires for us to do. Then our life gets out of balance, out of order, and we have chaos. No peace! We're frustrated, and in some cases we frustrate others—our spouse, our family, and even our friends. God wants us to have peaceful, orderly lives (Appendix A). He is a God of order (1 Corinthians 14:33).

If we want others to see Christ reflected in every area of our lives, we must view life from God's perspective, not from our fellow humans' viewpoint, which dictates that everything should "look" right. Have the right-sized family, the right job, and the right material possessions. But God's view is that whatever we have (i.e., whatever God has given us), we should use in ways that reflect how he is working in our lives. He needs to be *the* focus. What we do should not be a front for others but the meeting of realistic needs for our family and ourselves. Our needs should be in line with the priorities God has given us. Among other things, the Lord wants to be reflected in our attitudes, priorities, and intentions.

When we have the proper focus, we can have a sense of direction in our life. Do you have a sense of direction? It's not enough to have some vague idea of direction, especially as it relates to your overall purpose in life. Having a sense of direction or—to use a better word—*vision* for your life will allow you to put your life in order. When we have a proper focus, we can have a sense of direction in our life. Having direction, or *vision* for the bigger picture, will allow you to put your life in order.

The "secret" to the Great Wallendas' ability to make it from one end of their tightrope to the other was their focus. They could not look around to what was going on around them. They focused on the point that remained steady (the platform at the other end) and concentrated only on that point. We can have many things going on around us (job loss, new addition to the family, etc.), but our focus (on God) should never change. We need, like the Wallendas, to have a fixed, not a moving focus.

Similarly, our ultimate source of vision, or sense of direction, should come from God's Word, the Bible—God's spoken Word. It is entirely about vision. It is about a holy God defining reality for us, calling us out of our circumstances and toward that which is enduring, noble, full of hope, and eternal. Read Prov. 29:18a. What happens when we have no vision or sense of direction in our lives? We wander aimlessly. But if we have a sense of direction (born out of our purpose and vision), then we can be on our way to having a balanced life—an ordered life! When God is the center of your life (all you do), everything else will be properly focused.

Perhaps you don't sense direction in your life based upon God's Word. Perhaps the ways of God that we have talked about thus far are unclear or unfamiliar to you. Perhaps you don't know the Lord of whom I've been writing. Take a moment to read Appendix B at the back of this study. Learn how you can ask God to take care of your life today and forever as you put your trust in Him.

Perhaps you have trusted in Christ at some point in your life, but you are having difficulty in keeping God as your focus. Take some time to read Appendix C at the back of this study. Without Christ as the focal point of your life, no purpose or vision will ever seem worthwhile; and your life will have little order or meaning.

As we continue with this study, I want all of us to be particularly aware of one truth: Although we can and will make progress, life is never perfect. We don't always make all the right decisions and choices. We must write our plans in pencil and allow God to erase and make the necessary adjustments. (Psalm 138:8; 57:2) For our family, the birth of our first child Joey changed our world. He is now a grown man, but in the early days his diagnosis (cerebral palsy, epilepsy, mental retardation, and severe allergies) was challenging and difficult. Some days we didn't think we'd make it. We experienced days of frustration, failure, and exhaustion; others were filled with joy, accomplishment and delight.

We all have challenges in our lives. The way we deal with them will determine how we "finish the course" of life. Some days we will accomplish what we set out to conquer, and other days we won't even be close, but in balancing life, how we finish is all that counts.

Sometimes we need to stop and reevaluate where we are and where God wants us to be. He must be our focus! Life can be an exciting adventure when we know where we are going with it and who is with us to guide us!

Stop—Look—Listen

Today always comes before tomorrow.
Plan accordingly!

1. Why do we want a balanced life?

   - Look up 1 Corinthians 14:33. The context in which this verse was written provides us a glimpse into an early church service. The apostle Paul emphasizes the need for order in the church services. Why? Because that would be consistent with the nature of God, which reflects order and clear direction. By contrast, if disorder marred the church service, what would people say of the God who is worshipped? Let's now apply this to our own lives. Knowing that our God is a God of order, what are the implications of having a balanced life?

_____

_____

_____

_____

_____

- Observe the lesson of the ant from Scripture. Read Proverbs 6:6–11. What does the passage teach you? What attitudes, priorities, and intentions did both the ant and the grasshopper have? What was their vision? Their sense of direction?

_____

_____

_____

_____

_____

2. What does God see when He sees your:

   •   Attitudes:

   _____

   •   Priorities:

   _____

   •   Intentions:

   _____

   Are you headed for a goal? Do you see the big picture because of the clear vision you have? Are you balanced? Are you focused? On what are you focused?

3. What needs do you and/or your family have? List below. Then check the ones you believe God wants for you and/or you and your family.

   Your Needs

   •   _____

   •   _____

   •   _____

   •   _____

   •   _____

> Our greatest danger in life is in permitting
> the urgent things to crowd out the important.
> Charles E. Hummel (Tyranny of the Urgent)

4. The following are some things that keep us from doing what God wants us to do. Check all of the following that describe your present frame of mind. Read the verses and summarize the solution.

☐ I'm so busy. I feel as if I'm losing control! (Psalm 34:14)

_____

_____

_____

_____

☐ I am fearful. (Philippians 4:6–7; Matthew. 6:25–34; 1 Peter 5:7; Isaiah. 41:13)

_____

_____

_____

_____

☐ I am weak. I have little strength or endurance. (Psalm 73:26–28; Psalm 29:11)

_____

_____

_____

_____

☐ I procrastinate. (Proverbs 6:6–11)

_____

_____

_____

_____

☐ I do enough and want to take the break I deserve. (Job 15:31; Matthew 6:1–5; Hebrews 6:11)

_____

_____

_____

_____

☐ I am easily distracted. My eyes are off the Lord and consumed with people, things, and tasks. (2 Chronicles 16:9a; Is. 26:3)

_____

_____

_____

_____

☐ I am frustrated. (Psalm 29:11; John 14:27)

_____

_____

_____

_____

☐ I am afraid of failing. (Psalm 4:5; Psalm 16:8; Psalm 27:14; Psalm 37:3–5)

_____

_____

_____

_____

☐ I am anxious. (Isaiah 41:10)

_____

_____

_____

_____

☐ No one else is doing it *or* everyone else is doing it. (Romans 8:18; 2 Corinthians 10:12–13)

_____

_____

_____

_____

☐ I'm doing better than _____, so I'm not doing too badly. (2 Corinthians 10:12–13)

_____

_____

_____

_____

☐ I expect too much. (Philippians 2:14–15)

_____

_____

_____

_____

☐ I'm already doing very important things. (2 Corinthians 9:6–8)

_____

_____

_____

☐ It takes too much time to organize and plan.

_____

_____

_____

Next Step

Do you need a plan? Do you need to know where to go from here? Which of the previous excuses are you using? Are they legitimate? Become a problem solver!

1. Recognize the reason you lack a focus to balance your life. Describe it:

   _____

   _____

   _____

2. Realize you can solve some aspects of the problem and others, you can't. List them:

   Problems I can solve if I choose to take action:

   _____

   _____

   _____

   Problems I can't solve, but will pray about:

   _____

_____

_____

3. Look at what you can solve, and list several ways you
   will take steps toward a solution. (You may need to
   outline daily, weekly, and monthly steps. Don't outline anything beyond three or four months. Solutions
   must be divided into small, manageable steps so that
   you will see progress.)

_____

_____

_____

Fine-Tuning

Of the several ways you just listed under **Next Step #3**,
choose one that you will concentrate on specifically this
week:

_____

_____

_____

_____

On Your Own

The Tyranny of the Urgent! by Charles E. Hummel (Inter-Varsity Press) is a great read. Take a moment to read it online and consider placing orders for the booklets for yourself and to share with others.

Just for your own information and study, list those things you do this week that fall into the following categories:

Urgent (requiring immediate attention)

- _____
- _____
- _____
- _____
- _____
- _____
- _____
- _____

- _____
- _____
- _____

Important (having value)

- _____
- _____
- _____
- _____
- _____
- _____
- _____
- _____
- _____

Do any of the situations you listed above fall into both categories? Highlight or circle them.

Do you recognize a pattern for the way you live?

How can this exercise help you?

Are the urgent items always important?

Are the important items always urgent?

Write out and memorize 1 Corinthians 14:33.

_____

_____

_____

SESSION THREE
STARTING WITH MYSELF

Let's Get Started

List three qualities you see in yourself:

1. _____

2. _____

3. _____

Mark each item with a + if you think it is a positive trait and a - if you think it is a negative trait. We will refer to these items later in this lesson.

For which quality are you most grateful? Explain.

_____

_____

_____

_____

Today's Topic

In order to achieve balance and exercise discipline, we need to start with the self. If we have a poor self-image, then that faulty view will discolor all areas of our lives. A positive self-image means that we see ourselves as God views us. We will now look at how to develop a self-image with a divine perspective.

What Causes Problems with Our Self-Image?

1. Sinful Reasoning

   The Problem: When we process in our minds what is going on in life with sinful reasoning, then everything is distorted—our thoughts, motives, actions, attitudes, dealing with others, seeing things our way, creating stories to bend things in our direction, and eventually it affects our fellowship with God. Read from Romans 8:5–17 and share how this impacts your life.

The Solution: We all sin and have need for forgiveness (yes, even if we tell that little white lie or a half truth, say a nasty word, or exhibit a harsh attitude). The beauty of it all is this: God forgives and corrects. We just need to ask the Lord to forgive us and others and then allow God to work in and through us as we obey and yield to God's direction. When we read his word and take time to listen in prayer, he'll make clear our sinful ways. Read Romans 5:8 and tell what this verse means to you. Take a moment to look up Colossians 2:8. How does this apply to you?

_____

_____

_____

2. Lack of Purpose

The Problem: We feel no purpose in our lives, at our jobs, and in our homes, so we see ourselves as worthless. Sadly, the end result is that we are unhappy, and we can make those around us unhappy. Some take that worthlessness and slip into their own private pity parties, sulking, and—although it doesn't always lead here—it can ultimately find its way to depression. Ultimately we have to trust God. How can you trust God to give you purpose according to Romans 8:28–31?

The Solution: Ask God to impart this vision to us so that we might understand and glorify him in all we do. Try different ways to serve others and see what fits best in your life and with your gifts and personality. Stop pitying yourself and start moving forward. Begin serving, and your eyes will be open to see that there are others who have it worse than you. By your helping and serving others, you will begin to thank God for what you've been given. Start with prayer (and reading Philippians 4:5–8), and God will give you your next step. Are you ready and willing?

_____

_____

_____

3. Standards

The Problem: We allow the pressures and influences of this world and opinions of others to set our standards. The more we see what others have, the more we want, the more selfish we can become. We can also become jealous and envious—qualities that are not attractive, because they are sinful. Proverbs 23:17 cautions us.

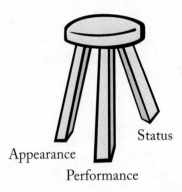

Appearance   Status

Performance

If appearance, performance, and status are the three legs holding up the self-image stool, what happens when one of the legs is pulled out? The job ends, our skills decline or our health wavers, and the stool falls. The same happens when we feel we are not meeting the standards (whatever the current standard is) in one of these areas. That standard will vary depending where we are in our life; thus, our self-image "doesn't have a leg to stand on," so to speak. Where will we look for our sense of identity and worth?

_____

_____

_____

The Solution: We must be able to stand alone with Christ, daily conforming to God's image, not that of the world. Colossians 1:28 gives us hope. It is important to surround yourself with others in your life who are a positive influence–those who will help you keep your self confidence and encourage you to continue in the right direction.

_____

_____

_____

4. Comparison

The Problem: We wrongly compare ourselves to others, wishing we had more of something in order to gain the approval of other people. The areas in which we most commonly make comparisons are the same three legs of the stool that make up our self image:

- Appearance—Our physical appearances as well as how we "make" things look that aren't accurate

- Performance—Our abilities, gifts, talents, etc.

- Status—Our job, our finances, etc.

Someone always has more than what we have, and someone always has less. Most of us compare our weakness with another person's strength; or vice versa. We will never attain a positive self-image that way. Challenge yourself by looking up the following verses: 2 Corinthians 10:12, 1 Samuel 16:7, Isaiah 53:2, and write out how these verses speak to you.

The Solution: We must compare ourselves to the person of Jesus Christ and seek his character for ourselves. One thing I've learned over the years is that we can't have everything at one time. We may have the finances to do certain things, but not the time. We may have freedom to do certain things but not the talent. Consider the ways you are making comparisons in your life, and see if this isn't true. Summarize 2 Corinthians 10:12:

_____

_____

_____

5. Failure

The Problem: We fear failure. None of us likes to fail because doing so seems shameful. Unfortunately, some people constantly watch and wait for our failure so they can use it against us. Other times we are the only ones who remember our own failure! And we can be harder on ourselves than those around us! Many times, though, failure can turn into achievement.

Failing chemistry my first quarter of college put my timely graduation in jeopardy. I needed three quarters of chemistry, and it was sequenced with other courses leading up to student teaching. Taking a chemistry class "audit" one summer to try to understand the concepts allowed me to gain enough confidence to get through those three courses needed. I was traumatized, but I endured.

I was actually able to graduate a quarter early and eventually interviewed with the superintendent of a small school system. The first question he asked me was, "Well, Cindi, I see you got an F in chemistry. How did *that* happen?" I was able to turn that failure into personal achievement by drawing on the lesson I had learned. I responded by saying, "I realize the F sticks out quite obviously, but if you look further you will see what I did to improve and that I did well in the courses I plan to teach. If you want someone with straight As (as I knew was the case with my competition), you'll have to hire someone else. If you want someone who has struggled and succeeded, a person who can help the student who just can't seem to 'get it,' then you can hire me. I'm prepared to help those who may struggle." A few days later I got the call, and the job was mine!

I've had other failures as well: moments in marriage, in parenting, in ministry, in friendships, in life.... but the beauty is that we can learn from these failures, if we are willing, and can grow from them. Read Isaiah 40:31 for encouragement.

The Solution: We need to look to God to meet us where we fail. His grace is sufficient. His strength overcomes any weaknesses we have. Are you willing to trust him? Will you surrender to him? Will you allow him to do a work in you so that others will see him through you? What does 2 Corinthians 12:9 say to you?

_____

_____

_____

How Can You Change Your Perspective to See Yourself from God's Point of View?

Realize your ungratefulness for how God made you or for situations given you, and express it here:

_____

_____

_____

In order to move beyond your ungratefulness, you need to write a prayer of confession here (Proverbs 28:13):

_____

_____

_____

Forsake your sin and old self-image (2 Corinthians 5:17).

_____

_____

_____

Give thanks to the Lord that he forgives and can change us. Accept how God made you (1 Thessalonians 5:18). (We are not always thankful for trials and hardships that God sends our way, but we can be intentional about giving thanks to the Lord as he helps us through the trials.)

_____

_____

_____

Repent by "turning away" from your sin, dedicate yourself to him, and allow him to conform you to his image (Romans 8:29; Luke 9:23). God helps us and also gives us other believers to help us.

We are made weak so that we can ask the help of others and not simply rely on our "self":

Write out what the following verses mean to you: 2 Corinthians 13:9, 11

_____

_____

_____

2 Corinthians 12:9–10

_____

_____

_____

We are made weak so that we can depend on others, not only our "self." Summarize the following:

Ephesians 2:10, 4:4

_____

Galatians 6:1

_____

1 Corinthians 12:14

_____

Romans 12:5

_____

1 Peter 4:7–11

_____

Remember that we are in the finishing process!

Philippians 1:6

_____

As you learn to see yourself from God's perspective, you will be victorious over many areas of your life. You should feel free to use the God-given gifts and talents you've been given, because you are using them for God's glory, not your own. Grant yourself the freedom to laugh and have fun. He gives us a sense of humor as a gift. Learn new activities to reenergize and motivate yourself for day-to-day living. Enjoy how God has made you! Read Ecclesiastes 5:18–20. It's a must!

"He has a right to interrupt your life. He is Lord. When you accepted him as Lord, you gave him the right to help himself to your life any time he wants." Henry Blackaby, *Experiencing God.*

Stop—Look—Listen

1. Knowing we need to develop characteristics worthy of a child of God, we must build trust in our Designer and develop a self-image with a divine perspective. It is the only way to achieve balance! The Scripture teaches us that we should not conform to the world. How can we successfully avoid conformity? Read Romans 12:2, and in your own words write out how you can avoid conforming to this world:

How should we view ourselves in light of God's works?

Psalm 139:14

_____

_____

Ephesians 2:10

_____

2. We briefly discussed the causes of problems with our self-image. Let's see what the Scriptures say about the solutions to each:

Sinful Reasoning:

Romans 5:8

_____

_____

Lack of Purpose:
Isaiah 43:7

_____

_____

1 Corinthians 6:20

_____

_____

Standards:
I Corinthian 4:16–18, 3:4–5

_____

_____

Comparison:
1 Samuel 16:7

_____

_____

2 Corinthians 10:12

_____

_____

Failure:
2 Corinthians 12: 9-10

_____

_____

3. Take a moment and go back to **Let's Get Started** and fill in this chart. We all have areas we need to improve. Every positive characteristic has a negative counterpart. List as many as you can think of.

Personal Traits	
Positive Traits (2 Corinthians 10:12; Philippians 1:6)	**Negative Traits** (2 Corinthians 12:9-10)
Very disciplined	Overly structured
Alert Flexible Humble	Nosy Indecisive Lacks confidence

_____

_____

That negative counterpart can become sinful if not put into proper perspective.

4. How does self-image tie into the idea of living the balanced life for you? Read Ecclesiastes 5:18–20.

_____

_____

_____

5. How much of yourself are you willing to give God? Tell him in a prayer:

_____

_____

Next Step

1. Recognize how a poor self-image has taken you off the track to a balanced life:

   * _____

   * _____

   * _____

2. Realizing that taking action cannot solve every problem, list below problems you have in terms of self-image that you can or cannot solve:

   Problems I can solve if I choose to take action:

   _____

   _____

   _____

   Problems I can't solve, but will pray about:

   _____

   _____

   _____

3. Considering what you can solve, list several ways you will take action:

- _____
- _____
- _____

Fine-Tuning

Look at what you listed in **Next Step #3,** and choose one that you will concentrate on specifically this week:

- _____

On Your Own

What character trait would you most like to work on?

_____

_____

_____

_____

Do you feel you are trying to control a particular area of your life? Name it:

_____

_____

Might God be asking you to allow him to take control of that area?

_____

_____

If God has all of you, you will make decisions that will affect an eternal perspective. You will not just live for the moment, hoping to gain what you can just for the here and now (looking to the temporal or temporary). You will have an eternal perspective. Do you believe you are looking to the eternal or to the temporal?

_____

_____

_____

_____

Is there someone who will hold you accountable in order to help you learn to balance your life? If so, who will it be?

_____

_____

Give that person a call, asking her or him to hold you accountable for six to eight weeks. Recommit at the end of that time if you both agree to it.

_____

_____

How can you avoid conforming to the world and instead transform to the likeness of Christ? Be specific. (Review Romans 12:2.)

_____

Example: If I _____, then I'll _____ Jesus Christ. (Example: If I stop being angry, then I'll reflect Jesus Christ.)

_____

_____

_____

Write out and memorize Romans 12:2.

_____

_____

_____

_____

SESSION FOUR
DISCIPLINE AND BALANCE

Let's Get Started

1. How would you define "discipline"?

_____

_____

Look it up and write out all of the definitions you find:

_____

_____

2. In what area(s) do you lack discipline?

- _____

- _____

- _____

3. Why do you think you lack discipline in those areas?

_____

4. Have you asked someone to hold you accountable? _____ If so, who? _____

Are you actively helping someone to be accountable to you? _____ If so, who? _____

_____

_____

_____

Today's Topic

Self-discipline is the outer reflection of an inward condition, manifesting itself as self-control—instant obedience to the initial prompting of the Holy Spirit.

Sometimes when we lack discipline, we look for the easy way instead of the best way. Perhaps we've never really learned to be disciplined. Then one area of little or no discipline spills over into another and then another and another until we have problems in many areas. Perhaps we lack discipline because we are passive, lazy, or disobedient to the Lord's leading.

Undisciplined people often develop poor self-images because they have not built trust in their Designer, Jesus Christ. This inward condition manifests outwardly, for instance, in a lack of discipline in spending money, failing to eat or exercise properly, or spending hours on the computer. Sometimes a lack of discipline manifests itself via indulgence, for example, buying impulsively with money we don't have, eating uncontrollably until it shows, desiring pleasure and play before the work is done. Many eventually see that lack of discipline has transferred to their children. The lack of discipline unfortunately can be learned by example, no matter how poor the example! And how can those of us who have children, expect them to learn discipline when we can't get a handle on it for ourselves?

This lack of discipline becomes so normal and commonplace in our lives that we have difficulty identifying or seeing it. We live with a problem so long that we don't even see it as a problem. Let me give you an example.

We had our kitchen ceiling repaired prior to moving into our home. We thought it had been properly fixed, because it looked fine. We moved in and put everything into use. Before long we found the real problem—something in the upstairs bathroom. The real problem had been ignored, so the same water problem persisted. We experienced the ceiling problem for the second time. The problem in the bathroom was repaired, and so was the kitchen ceiling. But now we had a drywall "dust" issue to deal with. It went far beyond the kitchen (if you know what I mean)!

Everything was fine for a while, but we eventually had a kitchen ceiling problem for a third time! Same bathroom, different problem. Again, repairs were done. But the *fourth* time something happened (same spot—*new* problem), I absolutely refused to have the repair done! I did *not* want the dry wall "dust" again! (I believe I told my husband we would move first.) So we lived with it for quite a while. I don't actually remember how long we lived with it, because it became a very normal sight to me. I was reminded of it only when first-time guests visited and their eyes were drawn to it. No one ever said or asked anything, and neither did I! Because we lived with the same problem every day, the problem became very normal to us.

My frustration with the problem caused me to quit fixing the problem. Various problems manifested themselves in the same place but always with different root problems. That's how it is with personal discipline in our lives! Our lives may lack discipline, and it shows; but what is the root problem? Sin is the root problem that causes us purposely or subconsciously to avoid working on the issues that will allow us to be disciplined. Do we deal similarly with a lack of discipline? Do we quit trying to fix the problem because we have lived with it so long that it actually becomes a *normal* part of our lives? Others may notice it but dare not say anything about it. And that just helps us overlook the—shall we say—"obvious"! Our lack of discipline could be rooted in a deeper, unseen, inward spiritual issue or problem that manifests itself in outward characteristics showing up in many areas of our lives.

So what can we do to put balance into our lives? I believe we must start with discipline.

The reason we find being disciplined so difficult is that many of us fail to do the following:

1. Have the *need* brought to our attention
2. *Recognize* our need for discipline
3. Have the *desire* to do something about it
4. Then take *action* to do something about it

In addition we must have the faith and hope necessary to get started. According to Hebrews 11:1, " ... faith is the assurance of things hoped for, the conviction of things not seen." If we lack hope, we have developed a negative mindset about ourselves; and have already lost the battle to become disciplined with no hope of becoming balanced.

The Wallendas did not practice their balancing acts at one hundred feet in the air; they practiced them two to three feet off the ground until they learned the discipline and skill that then gave them the confidence to perform their acts at greater heights. As Christians we must remember that we, too, must practice doing the lesser and smaller tasks before God gives us bigger responsibilities. If we have too much to balance, perhaps it's because we add too much before we have developed the required skills.

As Christians we believe our bodies to be the temple of the Holy Spirit (1 Corinthians 3:16–17; 6:19). We also know that our God is a God of order, that he is holy, etc.; yet some cling to the mindset that says, "I'll never be disciplined in my life." At this point we should immediately recognize a conflict in our Christian lives.

Why do these situations occur? How and why are these ideas implanted in our minds, resulting in defeatist mindsets? These ideas cause what is called a spiritual stronghold, that is, a mindset clogged with hopelessness that leads us to accept as unchangeable the situations we know are contrary to the will of God. Satan deviously builds strongholds in the believer's mind so that he can manipulate behavior without being detected. God counterattacks strongholds by renewing our minds (Romans 12:1, 2).

Only then will we be able to change and thus develop to be more Christlike. Discipline can be a wonderful quality, but it must be developed. We must ask ourselves, "What have we accepted as *normal?* Do we want to be satisfied with normalcy, or do we want to rely on Christ to give us hope, order, and self-control?" We must be willing to learn. We can become disciplined only by learning the wisdom of the Lord. A willing heart will find it exciting! (James 1: 5–8)

Stop—Look—Listen

1. Discipline is not an easy word to digest for most of us, but definitely a key word for our lives! Read Hebrews 12:10–11. Why does God discipline us?

    For our _____ and to share in his

    _____.

    Discipline at the moment seems _____, but it can yield _____!

    To whom? _____

2. A *lack* of discipline starts inwardly. How can we stop its growth? How can we see discipline take hold in our own lives? Summarize these two verses as you apply them to your own lives. (Be specific.)

    Philippians 4:6

    _____

    _____

Matthew 6:34

_____

_____

3. If we desire discipline and have difficulty reaching the next level, what must we do in order to develop a balanced life? Where do we find our direction? Write out Matthew 6:33:

_____

_____

4. Is it possible to make the changes we need to become disciplined in our lives? Read Romans 12:2 and tell why it *is* possible.

_____

_____

The only person you can control is you!

5. Discipline with God's wisdom can produce a balanced life. It will take one step at a time to develop the following:

- Peaceful Attitude
- Self-Respect
- Positive Self-Image
- Disciplined Life

—as we apply each one to every area of our lives: our bodies, souls, and spirits.

What if we feel we don't have God's wisdom? What should we do? Read and summarize James 1:5–8:

Where can we begin to understand balance and discipline? Summarize these verses:

Of what must we be careful? Ephesians 5:15–17:

_____

_____

Read Proverbs 9:10. What is the beginning of wisdom?

_____

_____

How do we gain understanding?

_____

_____

6. And what if we choose to reject the wisdom of the Lord? Read Proverbs 1:23–33 and summarize it in your own words as it applies to you.

_____

_____

Next Step

1. Recognizing where balance and discipline are lacking can be very helpful. Is your life well-balanced, are you tipping to one side, or are you not even on the balance? Let's begin by thinking about what aspects of our lives keep us occupied. Honestly consider each category and place a check mark in the column that best describes where you believe you are right now in your life.

My Life on Paper

Category	Not Even On The Balance	Balanced	Out Of Balance
Spiritual Life			
Family Relationships			
Friendships			
Hobbies/Recreation			
Finances			
Diet			
Exercise			
Work			
Church Ministry			
Future Opportunities			
Technology			
Television			
Other _____			

2. Read Proverbs 16:11 and put into your own words how the Lord deals with balance.

_____

_____

3. Taking each of the categories you listed above from your own life, make/sketch a wheel diagram that you *think* describes what your life is like. See the sample below:

Typical Weekly Time Allocation Chart

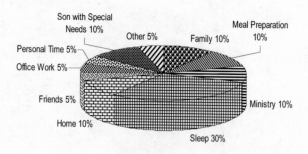

SAMPLE

YOUR WHEEL DIAGRAM

4. Of the aspects of your life that you believe are out of balance in one direction or another, list what you think you can solve, and what you believe is out of your control.

    _____

    _____

    Problems I can solve if I choose to take action:

    _____

    _____

    _____

    Problems I can't solve, but will pray about:

    _____

    _____

    _____

5. Of what you can solve, list several steps you will take to do so. Make sure you keep the steps small and simple:

_____

_____

_____

Fine-Tuning

Of the several ways you just listed under **Next Step #5**, choose one that you will concentrate on specifically this week:

_____

On Your Own

We will use the following Time Chart to fine-tune what you have already done on your basic wheel diagram by keeping track of all that you do with your time this coming week. At the end of the week, list each of your categories and add the total hours you put into each category. Make a new wheel diagram, showing the percentage of time you actually spent on each category. As you look at your new diagram, what can you learn from it? Did you spend as much time with your friends or family as you really thought you did? Did you have more or less free time than you originally thought? As I've had several opportunities to undertake this project, I'm reminded over and over that the things I *love* doing, I never seem to have enough time to enjoy, and the things that require a lot of effort require less actual time than it seems they do. Once you see the reality of the way you actually spend your time, you can evaluate changes that must occur to balance your life. Use this new diagram to fine-tune where you want to spend more time and where you want to find more balance. The key is this: "Am I doing what God wants me to do with the time given me?"

Write out and memorize Matthew 6:33:

_____

_____

_____

_____

Time Chart

Time	Sunday	Monday	Tuesday	Wednesday	Thurday	Friday	Saturday
12 am							
1 am							
2 am							
3 am							
4 am	Sleep						
5 am							
6 am	Get ready	Get ready					
7 am		Joey ready					
8 am		Laundry					
9 am	Get ready	Write					
10 am	Joey ready	Write					
11 am		Nap					
12 pm	CHURCH	Lunch					
1 pm	Lunch	Drive Joey					
2 pm	Relax						
3 pm							
4 pm							
5 pm		Cook					
6 pm	Cook	Dinner					
7 pm		Bible Study					
8 pm							
9 pm							
10 pm							
11 pm	To bed	To bed					

After completing your Time Chart for a full week, fill in your new wheel diagram with percentages of *actual* time spent in each category:

New Wheel Diagram - Percentages of Actual Time Spent in Each Category

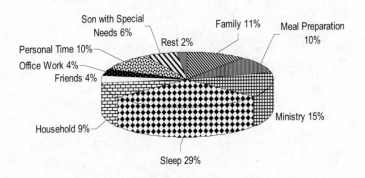

SAMPLE

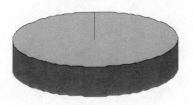

YOUR NEW WHEEL DIAGRAM

Share your circle diagram with others in your group or with the one to whom you are accountable during these sessions. Together ask and answer these questions:

What would make my circle diagram more ideal? Can you begin to find a "working routine"?

What were my presumptions of my schedule before doing this exercise?

What are my thoughts now about my actual schedule? Am I willing to make changes?

We will refer to your chart again in Session Six.

SESSION FIVE
GOALS—PART ONE
BASIC GUIDELINES

Let's Get Started

Read the *Rock Story* in Appendix D. Then answer the following questions:

_____

What do you consider to be the "big rocks" in your life?

- _____

- _____

- _____

List (but limit to four in each category) areas in your life where you feel:

Overcommitted
•
•
•
•

Overstressed
•
•
•
•

Overloaded
•
•
•
•

Some items may qualify to be listed under each category!

Today's Topic

As we work to become disciplined in our lives, we recognize the need to set goals. They can be elusive in our thoughts but concrete if we see them on paper day to day. I've always been a goal-oriented person because I like the feeling that comes from achievement, but it wasn't until I began raising a family that I needed to see my goals written on paper! The immediate demands of homemaking and childrearing blurred my vision of goal setting. Some days I felt as if I were holding on by a thin thread, trying to manage everything and keep a good attitude. I know many men who feel the same way as they juggle business, home, family, and ministry.

As I put into practice what I am about to share with you, most days were manageable, and each day had value and productivity. Goal setting takes discipline and work, but the end result is rewarding.

People without goals are similar to the main character in *Alice in Wonderland*. Alice was lost and asked the Cheshire cat whether he could tell her which way she needed to go. The cat said, "It depends on where you want to get to." It didn't matter to Alice, and the cat responded, "Then it doesn't matter which way you go." Isn't that how it is without goals? If we don't know or care where we're going, the chances are pretty good we won't get there, wherever *there* may be! If you aim at nothing, you will hit nothing every time! But if your goal is to glorify God, he needs to be the center of your life and the center of all that is in your circle diagram from the previous lesson!

Before we start to set some goals, let me introduce you to a few ground rules that I believe are essential to what we want to accomplish.

1. Be sure to have a daily quiet time of prayer and Bible reading. You must make a conscious decision to do so. If you do not partake of your spiritual food daily as you do of your physical food, you will not have strength or endurance for the day ahead. Just like we need daily food to grow and stay healthy, we need

God's Word. Read: Psalm 1:2; Mark 1:35; Psalm 5:3; 1 Timothy 4:15.

2. Get enough rest. Rest helps develop a right attitude as well as helps our bodies heal properly—physically, mentally, and emotionally! How much is enough? We are all different, but make the decision based upon your health, stage of life, number and ages of your children, and your endurance and energy levels. If you wake up each morning still tired, you probably need more sleep.

3. Know your boundaries and limitations. Limitations include what you do, for example, television viewing thirty hours a week and phone conversations that last hours that frustrate you and infringe on your personal time, as well as the limitations inherent in your own personality. What are the things in your personality that "set you off"? What is your energy level? Are you pushing it to its limits? When you know your limitations, you will make choices that will help you manage your time, your goals and scheduling, and your life in general. To quote John Wesley, "Though I never waste time, I am never in a rush because I never undertake more work than I can do with calmness of spirit." Knowing our limitations sometimes means we have to choose to eliminate certain things from our schedules. It usually boils down to whether or not you're willing.

4. Realize you can't have everything all at once. It simply isn't realistic! Of our resources of time, energy,

finances, and talents, seldom will we experience a time when we have it all, all at once. While in a furniture refinishing shop, I read a sign posted in a spot everyone could see. It said something like this: "You can have your furniture (1) finished in a short amount of time, (2) for a low cost, (3) with the finest of quality. Pick two." Let's look at that with a real life example. If you spent a lot of time at work (overtime), chances are that you have little energy and little time to invest in your talents. You may make more money and can even hire out to do tasks you don't have time to do, but you will still lack the time needed to be able to invest in using your talents in places other than work. As a mother at home full time, you may get all the housework done and save money by not hiring it out, but you lack the energy to spend the time you'd like with your children and have little or no time to develop your talents as you would like. Think of a few "real life" examples in your own life right now.

5. Be realistic! Keep your needs in mind. Focusing on your present needs, not perfection, is realistic. I often urge people at my seminars to plan a "buffer" time in their day. My husband Joe is a dentist. Although he is semi-retired now, when he worked full-time he planned into the daily work schedule a thirty minute "buffer" on the front side of the lunch hour. The buffer served several purposes. When unexpected changes, delays, or emergencies occurred, the extra half hour accommodated those interruptions. When

it wasn't needed, employees enjoyed a longer lunch. Mothers at home with young children usually get a kick out of trying to visualize just how they might plan that buffer period in their day. Actually, it is impossible to do it in the way I just described in my husband's office. But what I recommend is not packing so much into a day that there is little or no room for a child to have a skinned knee or to stop and give a hug just when you feel like it. I've had those days, so I know! I had to learn to plan my days in such a way that I had no back-to-back activities, one after another and with little or no time between. When my days were not thought out in terms of having a buffer time somewhere—anywhere—then when any tiny thing (interruption/surprise/crisis) happened, everything went crazy! The only way to plan a successful buffer in your day is to reread number three and make it an action point. Often!

6. Be a person of your word. This is a key to being reliable in all areas of your life. Your family, friends, and colleagues will know that they can count on you because you will remain true to your word. If you should then "forget" or make a "mistake," they will likely be more understanding because it's not your usual way. Let your "yes be yes and your no, no." Read Matthew 5:37 and Psalm 15:4c.

7. Follow a schedule. Once you decide how your chart will look, you will have a feeling of security. You can say "no" without feeling guilty, and you can say "yes"

with confidence. You won't take on too much, and you won't set yourself up for failure by letting your schedule take over. You will master your schedule. The most difficult part is "sticking to it"!

8. Do the most difficult tasks in your day first. It's easy to do what you enjoy at any time of the day even when you're tired. Saving the harder tasks until the end of the day usually results in taking them to bed with you at night and rising with them for yet another day! But you won't do tasks you don't enjoy doing when you've had a long day and you are tired.

9. Learn to say "no"! Saying "no" shouldn't have anything to do with how busy we are. It should have everything to do with our priorities, goals, purposes, and responsibilities. Before you say "yes" to anything, ask yourself the following questions:

- Are my working hours in line with my family life (needs and decisions) and season of life?

- Does my work/life schedule set a good example to my family, friends, and colleagues?

- Do I have room for this in my schedule?

- How will this affect my family, myself, and others around me?

- Will this cause unnecessary stress?

- What is the full extent of the commitment?

- Am I using the gifts that God has given me, or is this "out of my league"?

- Is someone else able to do this or perhaps better able or gifted to do it?

- Why do I think I want to do it? What is the motivation?

Review Appendix E for a full list of questions to ask yourself, your spouse, and your children to help you determine what can be added to your schedule and what should be removed.

Ask questions and pray about each; then you are ready to give an answer.

10. Know your responsibilities. Do the things you know are yours to do. Do not take over the responsibilities of others in your home, at work, or even in ministry. At times you need to help out. I am not talking about that. I am talking about "taking over." When you take over the responsibilities of others, you are silently saying that they can't do their job, that you can do it better, or that you want control of this area. All are dangerous and lead to the frustration of both parties. In addition, this is one of the main reasons we find our schedules getting out of control.

Having a grown son with special needs keeps us ever mindful of the responsibilities we have to him. Those responsibilities carry over to every decision we must choose to make. Such decisions are not always popular with others, but we must chose to do what works best for our particular situation, and so must you.

11. Reevaluate your goals yearly, monthly, and even daily, if necessary. Those who have small children may need to reevaluate their goals by the minute! The idea is to review often enough that you feel you can make the changes necessary to maintain a balanced life. It's a challenge, but revisiting those goals will often help you keep the focus you need (eyes on Jesus and His will for your life), and the balance you desire. Empty nesters may need to reevaluate and change their goals less often, but to continue establishing balance it will need to be done.

Before continuing this study, read Appendix F.

Stop—Look—Listen

> Sow a thought and you reap an act; sow an act and you reap a habit; sow a habit and you reap character; sow a character and you reap a destiny. Charles Reade

1. The most important consideration at the outset of goal-setting is to reserve a consistent daily time for prayer and reading God's Word. Without a commitment to a daily quiet time, all efforts to set goals, manage time, and balance your life will be squan-

dered. How often do you observe a quiet time? When should you have a quiet time? Look up the following Scripture verses and put them into your own words:

- Psalm 1:2

_____

- Mark 1:35

_____

- Psalm 5:3

_____

- Joshua 1:8

_____

If you don't have a daily quiet time, *when* and *what* will you do to improve?

_____

2. It is important to realize that proper rest is restorative to our emotional, physical, and spiritual well-being. Proper rest helps us see our goals through.

With these thoughts in mind, answer the following questions:

Do you feel you are getting enough rest?

How many hours (in a row) are you sleeping?

If it's too much or not enough, what is your plan?

If you lack sleep, how do you feel it affects setting and achieving your goals?

3. After each of the resources listed below, circle high, medium, or low to indicate the amount you think you have at this stage of your life:

Resource	Amount		
Time	High	Medium	Low
Energy	High	Medium	Low
Finances	High	Medium	Low
Talents	High	Medium	Low

Even though we all have the same twenty-four hours in our day, we may feel that we could use more time. But as you decide what you should circle, be realistic. I know that natural inclination to want more of each of the resources listed above, but because it won't realistically happen, we need to learn to balance what we have—what the Lord has given us.

Now that you have circled your responses, how do you feel each area has changed from five years ago? How do you think each will change in the next five to ten years? Why is it important to try to balance each?

_____

_____

Do you think it will be helpful to set goals for these and other areas based upon the changes you have and will experience?

_____

_____

4. Realizing that goal-setting is crucial to accomplishing tasks is important, but what about those times in our lives when emergencies take up the bulk of our time, energy, and even finances? How can we *realistically* balance the difference between our goals (even if we believe they are God-given) and what happens to us, especially those things over which we have no control? Look up the following verses to formulate your answer:

- Proverbs 27:1

_____

_____

- Matthew 6:34

_____

_____

- Proverbs 16:11

_____

_____

- Psalm 138:8

_____

_____

Next Step

1. Recognizing that part of our problem in goal-setting is in the daily disciplines, rate yourself on the following:

Daily Disciplines Chart

Daily Disciplines	Needs Work									Doing Well
Daily Quiet Time	1	2	3	4	5	6	7	8	9	10
Enough Rest	1	2	3	4	5	6	7	8	9	10
Know My Limitations	1	2	3	4	5	6	7	8	9	10
Keep Realistic Needs In Mind	1	2	3	4	5	6	7	8	9	10
Keep My Word	1	2	3	4	5	6	7	8	9	10
Follow A Schedule	1	2	3	4	5	6	7	8	9	10
Do Difficult Jobs First	1	2	3	4	5	6	7	8	9	10
Know When To Say No	1	2	3	4	5	6	7	8	9	10
Know My Responsibilities	1	2	3	4	5	6	7	8	9	10
Reevaluate Goals As Needed	1	2	3	4	5	6	7	8	9	10

2. Realizing there are some things about goal planning that may or may not be able to be solved, answer the following:

_____

_____

Problems I can solve if I choose to take action:

_____

_____

Problems I can't solve, but will pray about:

_____

_____

3. Considering what you can solve, list several ways you can take action:

- _____

- _____

- _____

Fine-Tuning

Of the several ways you just listed under **Next Step #3**, choose one to concentrate on specifically this week:

- _____

On Your Own

What are you living for?

_____

_____

_____

What is most important to you? What is keeping you from what is most important to you?

_____

_____

_____

Do you live as though what is most important is most important?

_____

_____

_____

Do you have a direction in life? What is it?

_____

_____

_____

How do your answers to the above questions go along with what Paul wrote in Philippians 3:13–14; Colossians 1:28–29?

_____

_____

Write out and memorize Proverbs 27:1:

_____

_____

_____

SESSION SIX
GOALS—PART TWO
ORGANIZING A SYSTEM

Time management is goal management.

Let's Get Started

1. If you have a "system" for scheduling your time, tell how it helps:

    • _____

    • _____

Tell how it does not work as well as you'd like:

• _____

2. If you do *not* use a schedule, system, or calendar, how do you survive?

_____

_____

3. After reviewing your time chart from Session Four, how do you feel you waste time?

_____

_____

4. After reviewing your time chart from Session Four, how do you feel you make good use of your time?

_____

_____

Today's Topic

A goal is the end result that a person aims to reach or accomplish. It is focused on the future, not on mistakes of the past. It focuses on results—specific results.

When Joe and I were first married, we decided to plan for two things. The first was a budget. The second was taking a moment at the beginning of each year and planning yearly goals. At first we just talked about them, but at some point we began writing them down (simply on a piece of notebook paper) so we would see them often and be reminded of the goals we had discussed. The interesting thing is that with rare exception we have achieved each goal.

> We reached most goals, not because they just "came to us," but because we could see them on paper, plan for them as needed, and acknowledge the small steps necessary to achieve the end result throughout the year. Here are the areas we discuss each year:

Goals for the Year _____

Personal:

Spouse/Marriage:

Family/Children:

Business/Work:

Ministry/Outreach:

Leisure/Relaxation/Rest:

Financial/Savings:

Character Traits:

Special Project:

As you set goals, follow these guidelines. Add others as they apply to your own life.

_____

_____

Determine your main purpose in life. I believe our main purpose as Christians, according to Isaiah 43:7, is to glorify our Heavenly Father. When we determine to set a goal that *all* we do will glorify God, we can set our goals more clearly and easily. Saying "yes" and "no" to tasks we are asked to do should become easier if they do not help to fulfill our purpose in life.

Pray about the goals you believe God would have you to set. Without an attitude of prayer, our goals tend to become selfish. Ask God what he wants you to do, who he wants you to become, and give him the freedom to do it in the way he may choose. As you read Romans 12:1–2, what stands out to you?

Set goals to motivate you. We wanted to be sure to set goals that motivated us! We all love doing things we enjoy. Setting goals in which we have no interest sets us up for failure immediately. Some goals may not be as motivating as others, but be sure you are excited about them. God's calling on our lives is generally something that excites and motivates us.

Set attainable goals and take action. We would never have set goals far beyond what we could reach. Twenty years into his dental practice, Joe's business projections were different than when he started. It took baby steps to reach where he wound up when he sold the practice after thirty-one years. Likewise, we would never set for ourselves goals to suit a family ten years ahead of us. Goals must be "attainable"; otherwise, we won't bother to follow through with trying to achieve them. The frustration level would be too high!

Make sure you can measure the progress of each goal and watch for results. Being able to measure your progress gives you a sense of accomplishment. Enjoying the success, you don't mind setting new goals to replace the ones you've achieved. Your results keep moving you forward.

Reevaluate unattained goals? Did a change in your life make it impossible to achieve (an unexpected addition to the family? a loss to divorce or death, etc.?) Also, I have found that goals need to be reevaluated often when children are little. Much changes often with little ones, and although you might like to plan for the year, planning quarterly (and sometimes daily) is more realistic and less frustrating! (Read

Genesis 1:25 and Genesis 2:18 to see how God evaluated his work.)

It's time to establish a "system." (For those who would like more information on home organization, visit our website for *Get it Together.)* The simplest method is working from a calendar. If you are single, you will use one just for yourself; but if you are married and if children enter into the picture of your life, you will need *one* calendar from which you all work. We can call it "central scheduling," and it must be kept up to date by one person (or all family members), and it must be kept in one place. Pocket calendars, Day-Timers, cell phones, and the various computerized devices can be used by the individuals in your family, but a central scheduling system is necessary to maintain order and harmony for everyone.

Here are a few of the rules we follow in keeping our "central scheduling" daily calendar:

- As soon as you know the dates (verbally or in writing) for whatever work, school, athletic, social, church (etc.) engagements you know you will accept (commit to), the dates must be put in ink on the calendar immediately. Make sure the location and time are on the calendar, too. If you put all the information on the calendar, you can throw out the informational paper, thus never having that item in your hands again.

- Use pencil to indicate dates and activities that are unconfirmed. If something else comes along on the date in question, simply make a call regarding the first activity. Once an activity is confirmed, write it in ink. Anything written in ink takes first priority and should not be changed for something "better" that might come along. Remember to make your "yes" a "yes"! What does Matthew 5:37 and Psalm 15:2–4 mean to you?

- When all our children lived at home, we asked twenty-four-hour notice (minimum) for "last minute" schedule changes or additions. Doing so allows time to be sure that we have all of the information needed: details of the time, the ride situation, calling to verify proper supervision, etc. If twenty-four-hour notice isn't provided, the answer is likely to be "no." Try it! Your pre-teens and teenagers will develop great scheduling techniques!

- Mark prayer requests for others in small print on your calendar. You will be able to remember and pray for others when they or their family members have special occasions, surgeries scheduled, etc.!

- Be sure to mark all doctors' appointments, meetings, weddings, birthdays, anniversaries, field trips, Bible studies, family events, work obligations, etc., on your main calendar. If it doesn't get to the calendar, you aren't likely to remember it! Don't rely on doctors' receptionists, friends, etc., to remind you. You must assume responsibility for your own commitments.

Below you may add suggestions that others in your group have found helpful.

_____

_____

Stop—Look—Listen

> Reaching your goal is not as important as what you are becoming in the process.

1. In questions three and four of **Let's Get Started**, you were asked to list how you waste time and how you make good use of your time. List below as many examples as you can to show that time-wasters can also become successful time-fillers in some situations.

Time - Wasters	Time -Fillers
Talking for a long time on the phone to "visit"	Talking on the phone while folding laundry
Reading a book when "pressing needs" aren't done	Reading while waiting at the doctor's office

The point I hope to make is that no matter how we spend our time, we can either waste it or use it wisely. We need to master this area so true time management and a balanced life can become our realities.

2. Please refer to the Year at a Glance in Appendix G. We will use this sheet to set general goals. Setting goals will help you organize your time. The first item you need to determine and fill in is what you believe your purpose in life to be. After determining what your purpose in life is (which is a general statement), you can then choose three specific goals to help you achieve what your main purpose in life is. A specific goal may be to teach Bible study, get a college education, or raise a family. Once you decide upon those three specific goals, you will be able to know what to say "yes" and "no" to in your everyday life. Don't even consider putting things on your chart that don't align with your main purpose in life and your three goals. You need not say yes to anything that doesn't match your goals and the purpose God has set before you! And you need

not feel guilty because it is God's purpose for you! God doesn't require of you what will be required of the rest of your family or your friends. You have a purpose designated by God and your goal is to obey. If you choose to start this now, fill in *only* the goals for next month. At the end of each month, you may fill in the upcoming month. Don't plan to fill out the whole year at once. If you take this chart to heart, you will be amazed at what you will accomplish in one year, with the proof because it is before you in your own writing!

3. Take a look at your chart from Session Four (how you spend time all day each day). Considering how you believe you wasted time and considering what the "big rocks" are that you want to put into the "jar" of life, fill out the next chart with items you *know* are worthy of your time. Any extra timeslots can be used for the things that you might like to do but are not of utmost importance to you based upon your life's purpose and specific goals (i.e., the gravel, sand, and water of life).

Time Chart

Time	Sunday	Monday	Tuesday	Wednesday	Thursday	Friday	Saturday
12 am							
1 am							
2 am							
3 am							
4 am							
5 am							
6 am							
7 am							
8 am							
9 am							
10 am							
11 am							
12 pm							
1 pm							
2 pm							
3 pm							
4 pm							
5 pm							
6 pm							
7 pm							
8 pm							
9 pm							
10 pm							
11 pm							

- How will you successfully accomplish the above?

_____

_____

_____

- Will someone hold you accountable to your plans?

_____

_____

_____

- After you've made a plan, try it for a full week and record your thoughts:

_____

_____

_____

> Important activities don't make your life more
> meaningful; a meaningful life makes
> your activities important.

Next Step

1. Recognize what organizing, scheduling, or prioritizing problems have gotten you off-track in managing your time and balancing your life and list them below:

- _____

- _____

- _____

Ask yourself these questions about each item you listed:

☐ Have I asked the Lord if this is an area that he wants me to set a goal(s) to achieve?

☐ Can I identify appropriate meaningful goals to set?

☐ Are they attainable?

☐ Can I measure the progress toward the achievement of these goals?

☐ When will I reevaluate these goals?

2. Problems I can solve if I choose to take action:

_____

_____

_____

Problems I can't solve but will pray about:

_____

_____

_____

3. Considering what you can solve, list several ways you can take action:

- _____

- _____

- _____

Fine-Tuning

Of the several ways you listed under **Next Step #3**, choose one that you will concentrate on specifically this week:

- _____

On Your Own

What activities make your life meaningful?

_____

_____

Do they fit with what you believe is your purpose in life?

_____

_____

How do those activities align with the goals you have set to accomplish your main purpose in life?

_____

_____

Write out and memorize: Philippians 1:6:

_____

_____

_____

_____

SESSION SEVEN
TIME FOR RELATIONSHIPS

Let's Get Started

1. Are you a better talker or listener? Or both? With regard to this question, describe yourself in two to three sentences.

_____

_____

_____

2. For you to have a meaningful relationship with someone (spouse, child, family member, friend, coworker), what needs to take place?

- _____
- _____
- _____

3. Is there a relationship that causes strife or awkwardness in your life at this time? Describe the relationship (family, friend, coworker, etc.) and what you believe has caused the strife or awkwardness.

_____

_____

Are you praying to be sure you're handling things properly? Are you staying away from gossip that will just make matters worse?

_____

_____

Today's Topic

On January 20, 1979, I wrote these words to myself in my Bible next to Romans 12:10–16, "Always have time for others, even if they don't have time for you." It has been a challenging goal! At times I have reached out and met a wall of silence or protection, or a wall that took more effort and energy to climb than I was able. Often I have made time for others, only to meet frustration, acknowledging that I was carrying the heavy lopsided load of that so-called friendship. When we experience these disappointments, it seems easier not to bother building relationships. And some people stop there. Disappointment allows no room to let anyone in. But as I reread the scripture and note to myself, I realize I cannot quit without having made some effort. At least I would be certain I had done what God asked me to do.

In today's society it is easy to shut everyone out. We open and close our garage doors without getting out of the car. We have air conditioning so we keep our windows and doors closed even when it's nice outside. We can't hear our neighbors, and they can't hear us. Some people have yard servicers to mow their lawn and do yard work. We have fences. We have dryers so we don't need to put our clothes outside on a line to dry. These examples reduce opportunities to wave to, say hello to, share conversation with, or even meet our neighbors. Some of us couldn't even identify our next-door neighbors if they were in a police lineup!

It's sad to say, but the same things are happening in some churches. Many relationships remain on the "surface." We don't know what others' needs are, what they are feeling, or what difficulties they experience. Nor do we know what brings them joy and in what they are rejoicing! Even sadder is that some of our own immediate family relationships are merely superficial. Do we have any idea what is going on in others' lives, in their hearts? Do others know or care about what is going on in our lives and hearts?

All of us are busy! But are we too busy to take time for our family, our friends, and those with whom we work? Is the effort really that great, or are we just not trained to seek others out? Or are we simply selfish, wanting our own needs met and forgetting the needs of others? Do we really even want to "connect" with others? When we (or others) have an urgent need, how long do we think anyone wants or *can* wait until someone comes alongside to help and comfort? Does is take too much energy? Or is it that some relationships are just too draining?

All of us have needs and want to share those needs with others. It helps lighten the load. But if we are shut off or shut up a time or two, we begin to make safe choices. Many times that safe choice is silence. But that kind of silence never satisfies. (Philippians 2:1–4).

We relate with others in many different ways: husband to wife, parent to child, friend to friend, grandparent to grandchild, etc. Each one has different relationships, characteristics, and boundaries. For instance, some conversations shared by a husband and wife should not be shared with friends; conversations shared by parents should not be shared with children, etc.; however, I believe a common biblical thread is woven through each relationship. That common thread is *love*. As we read 1 Corinthians 13, we learn what every *healthy* relationship requires: mutual caring, trust (honesty), and respect.

In order to survive our times, instead of drifting farther apart and closing ourselves off from others, we need to draw closer together. That won't happen merely by *hoping* for it. Developing relationships requires a lot of effort, trust, and time. We need to determine whether spending the time that's needed to develop a relationship is available to us. We may need to "find" time to develop relationships if we feel that area is lacking in our lives. Most relationships develop and deepen in time. They weather the storms of varying circumstances, disappointments, and frustrations. Trust is built. We move from familiarity with people to commitment to them in a deeper relationship.

Many good books are available to help us learn about differences in people and personalities and the way we each express ourselves in relationships. One thing I have learned is that all relationships must have an element of T.E.A.M. work (Together Each Accomplishes More). We must give and take, talk and listen, encourage and reprove, help and accept help. When only one person gives, listens, encourages, and helps, a relationship cannot flourish. Learning how to develop friendships, experiencing a great marital relationship, and knowing how to treat others must originate in the family. That is where we should learn *how* to do these things, and what to expect from others if we desire to be a part of healthy relationships.

Below is a chart showing the qualities I believe are important in developing each aspect of a relationship. If someone asks intimate and personal questions of someone whom they have just met or with whom they are only minimally familiar, developing a healthy two-way relationship may be difficult. We must build upon each of these steps in order to develop trust in others, in order to be transparent and real to others.

We cannot jump into a committed and faithful relationship without all the steps in between. We move from having a casual and familiar relationship to a committed and faithful relationship as we go through each step by spending time together and gaining confidence in the relationship at each level. As we take the time, we learn about each other's sense of humor, how well we each listen to each other, how we give and take, how we respond to different things, how we can pray and be available for each other. Each level of relationship involves give and take. I cannot expect of a friend anything that I would not be willing to do as well. In addition, if I am not receiving, I cannot expect the relationship to flourish.

Building Relationships

	Nature of the Relationship	Quality of the relationship	Actions to take in the relationship
COMMITTED ⇧ Only a few people will reach this level with us because of the depth of the relationship.	• Committed • Faithful • (Spiritual)	• Discover each other's strengths and weaknesses • Open and transparent communication • Freedom to listen, speak and act • Committed to confidentiality	• Able to encourage, correct, confront and help them reach goals and dreams
CULTIVATING ⇧ Fewer relationships in our lives get to this level.	• Feeling (Emotional)	• Enjoy similar interests • Plan things in common to enjoy together • We "click"	• Spend time together getting to know them • "Dig" deeper into the relationship, cultivating growth (asking and answering the why questions)
CASUAL ⇧ A great number of relationships in our lives fall into this category.	• Intellectual • Factual • Familiar • Casual (Mental)	• Know casually. • See occasionally • Usually unplanned meetings	• Learn about them through initial introduction and conversations • Asking and answering unobtrusive questions (who, what, where) to get to know them

I have not mentioned various kinds of relationships specifically because most of us desire many of the same things (someone to talk to, someone to listen, someone who enjoys some of the things I do); however, I need to make a few comments about the marital relationship. I believe spouses should work hard at being each other's best friend. Developing friendships should continue to be a very important part of each of our lives, but if marriage partners meet their needs for companionship/ friendship outside their marriage, it can be very dangerous. We must exercise caution to develop and maintain the marital relationship. No married person should engage in friendships with members of the opposite sex or spend time alone or in intimate conversations them. Even prayer with someone of the opposite sex may seem like a safe place, but we may enter into areas of intimacy in prayerful conversation that should be held specifically between the individual and the Lord or the individual and his or her spouse.

I am so thankful that Joe and I are not only husband and wife but also close committed friends. I wouldn't dream of making a major decision without him. And because of our friendship, we enjoy being in on all the little decisions as well. We enjoy spending time alone together. We love being with our immediate family as well as extended family, and we cherish time together with our dear friends; yet we each have individual friendships that hold us accountable to our relationship with God and others. Each of these relationships help us to balance our own lives. The healthy relationships help nurture and build Christlikeness in each person involved. The health of each relationship is an overflow of a healthy relationship with God. In order for that healthy relationship to grow with others, we need to grow a healthy relationship with our heavenly Father. Likewise, if we have a healthy and strong relationship with God, we will be keenly aware of unhealthy relationships that we have.

One reason I believe we are blessed with various relationships is that we have spent time nurturing them. We have found, however, that at different times in our lives, we have invested differing amounts of time in those friendships. We must balance the time spent on those within our home and those outside of our home. If we spend no time developing friendships when we have small children or even school-aged children at home, what will we expect to happen when they leave? It will be the friendships we have cultivated over the years that will fill the need for relationships when we have an empty nest. By the same token, what can we expect if we spend all of our time nurturing our friendships and neglect our own families? In some cases only time will tell. In other cases, I think we can learn from the experience and mistakes of others by learning how to balance relationships. Doing so is often difficult because some people will never be satisfied with the way relationships are balanced. Some will want more time, and others might wish to be left alone. Part of the balance is learning how to nurture relationships (review previous chart). Part of the balancing act is to know when you have spent too much time and energy on a friendship and need to realize it simply isn't going to work.

Self-centered people are unable to have healthy, flourishing relationships. Their selfishness will keep them from healthy relationships, and they find themselves going from one unhealthy relationship to another.

People like this need to learn to be controlled, directed, and empowered by the Holy Spirit of God. They need to surrender control to God instead of taking the control for themselves. (Review Appendix C if needed.)

In contrast, the person who develops healthy relationships *is* controlled, directed, and empowered by the Holy Spirit. Because God is in control, this type of person will have qualities in her or his life that reflect the character of God. This Spirit-driven/Spirit-led person has characteristics that look something like this:

- Desires the best for others

- Helps, encourages, is considerate of, and serves others (Ephesians 4:32)

- Is willing to sacrifice personal desires to do for others

- Acknowledges she or he has sinned and asks forgiveness

- Studies God's Word to understand his will for *all* areas of life

If you were choosing a friend, a mate, or a coworker, which would you choose? Which are you?

_____

_____

Stop—Look—Listen

Would I be willing to cancel my planned activity at a moment's notice if someone had an urgent legitimate need?

1. Read Matthew 7:12. What would you want others to do or be for you?

_____

_____

_____

Are you willing to make the time to do or to be the same for others?

_____

_____

_____

2. Look around you—at neighbors you know, friends you have, perhaps people in this small group or class. Then read Romans 12:9–21. How can you apply these verses to the following questions?

What needs do you see in their lives? How could you help meet those needs?

_____

_____

_____

How do you generally relate to others in a friendship? (Check one) Discuss.

☐ Interested in others but don't seek or pursue close relationships

☐ Interested in others and ask questions to get to know them

☐ Interested in others, ask questions to get to know them, and meet needs as appropriate

- [ ] Not interested in developing relationships/friendships beyond what I have

- [ ] Not interested in developing relationships

Would your answers change if you were asked how you generally relate in your marriage or family relationships? What does this tell you about yourself and how you relate? What does it tell you about the priority of relationships in your life? Do you have the balance you desire?

_____

_____

Read Philippians 2:20–21. How can you apply this verse to what you checked above?

_____

_____

3. For some people, pursuing friendships or relationships is difficult. For others, it's difficult to be pursued. Still others do not know how to be a friend or may have trouble maintaining friendships. Whatever our personality, at times we need to step out of our usual routine—our comfort zone—and take some chances. These involve

risks, but if we make no effort to develop relationships, we receive no blessings either. Why is it important to take time, to make time for relationships? How do you come to a point of balance between maintaining healthy family relationships, keeping close friendships, and developing new friendships?

_____

_____

Developing friendships is sometimes difficult if we are not used to one-on-one conversations for any length of time. In an era where social networking is the rage, we can connect without ever seeing someone face to face. This virtual reality has numbed us to deepening relationships—we build networks instead of friendships. It's often difficult to communicate in a real face-to-face conversation. I often witness conversations (sometimes my own) where two people are talking about themselves, and neither has inquired of the other. In many settings we go from one person to the next simply asking, "How are you?" and getting a mechanical "Fine, how are you?" in return. The uneasiness resulting from going beyond that trivial question is a stumbling block for many people. Is it for you? Perhaps that uneasiness can be taken away or at least decreased by mentioning a few hints for general conversation and then taking some time to write a few questions to use in conversations to overcome that hurdle. Why do we need to learn this? We must learn to recognize that each person that enters our life is an "appointment" from God! That is what makes relationships worth the risk! If we wonder how we will benefit from the friendship, we are already thinking the wrong way! We must view this person as important from God's perspective and desire to teach and be taught in and through this relationship. How can we help each other grow? That should be our ultimate goal in any healthy relationship.

One challenge I enjoy is learning something new about someone I have known for a long time. It is especially fun if it is something I have learned about a close friend, my husband, or even one of the children. Will you take that challenge in your life? Start by thinking of questions you would like to be asked or wouldn't mind being asked in a casual setting. As you gain confidence in learning new things about people you've known for a long time and are comfortable with, then begin venturing off into new relationships to learn about them. Consider that you might be asking these questions to people you have just met, or to those you would like to get to know better. First, remember a few hints that will help things go more smoothly.

Helpful Hints:

- A great place to start is to ask others about themselves—that which they know best. (Say to yourself, "This person, not me, is the key!")

- Don't ask intimate, personal questions of people you are meeting for the first time or are familiar with as only a casual acquaintance. A level of trust must be developed first.

- Be a good listener as the other person answers what you have asked. You will then know how to follow up with additional questions or comments, by asking things about the answer you've received.

- Ask questions that require more than a "yes" or "no" answer if you want to further any conversation.

Let's list four questions that you will be able to use in a casual setting to start and keep conversations going. Consider topics related to work, family, school, interests (church, hobbies, music, sports, or other skills). They will be factual or intellectual in nature. I'll give you two and you can add others:

- Are you originally from this area? (Follow-up questions: where, how long, etc.)

- What activities do you and your family (or friends) enjoy? (Follow-up questions: Camping sounds like fun! Where do you camp?)

- _____

- _____

List four questions that will allow you to move from a casual or familiar relationship to cultivate a closer companion and friendship relationship. Your questions will involve the emotional level (asking "why" questions) as opposed to asking factual questions. I'll start you with two and you can add others:

- Why did you quit your job? (Follow-up question: How do you feel about that?)

- Why are you afraid of heights? (Follow-up questions: Do you think you could ever conquer that fear?)

- _____

- _____

Let's now list four questions that you will be able to use in a closer, more committed relationship. A certain level of openness and trust must be determined. If the other person is not open to answering somewhat more intimate and personal questions, *you will not be able to proceed in that relationship.* If she or he is elusive (not open and honest) in answering, you can, at best, go back only to the cultivating relationship. Those questions will be of ethical, moral, or spiritual context (regarding personal or public opinions) and may include the person's faith or relationship with God. If you want this relationship to be the closest of relationships, it will entail getting involved in his or her life—correcting, confronting, and helping. By asking these types of questions, you will go beneath the "surface." I will give you two questions, and you can add others:

- What goals do you have for your own personal life? Do you feel you are achieving them? How can I help?

- How are you doing on your weight-loss program?

- _____

- _____

As we pursue a balanced Christian life, establishing balance in our relationships is important. In fact, one of the key strategies for a growing, maturing (balanced) disciple of Christ is establishing a *relational network* in his or her life. See the model below:

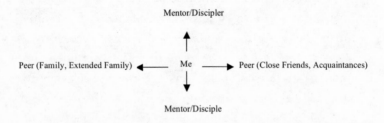

Each of us has a need to develop this relational network to be held accountable for our actions and attitudes. It is important to have someone who can and will help us through the trials and temptations from which no one is exempt! Powerful and successful Christian leaders have sinned and failed because no one held them accountable to a growing and balanced Christian life. Read Proverbs 27:17 to understand how God wants us to help one another.

Referring to the model above, we see that we need others in various aspects of our life so that we will be accountable in every aspect of our life. We must keep no secret places for sin in our lives. Mentoring is a relational experience in which one person helps another by sharing what she or he has learned in life. This includes guiding and coaching through wisdom, experiences, habits, and learned principles. A mentor is one who has gone before you and who can give you direction, encouragement, perspective, and reproof when necessary. Even if you are well established in ministry and in life in general, you will need someone in this capacity to help you to get to the next step that God has for you. This type of mentoring can take place over a long period of time or might occur with individuals who come and go in your life as you have made decisions or experienced transition, but they have made an impact on your walk with the Lord. Who is currently mentoring or has mentored you in your life?

One who would play the part of discipler in your life is one who can teach and train you through the scriptures as you grow in your relationship to Christ. As someone has done that for you, you then are able to teach and train another to help them grow from convert to discipler to worker to leader. Have you been discipled? By whom? Who have you discipled? Whom are you presently discipling? Read 2 Timothy 2:2 to see the natural by-product of this relationship.

This network includes all the people in your life and sphere of influence. You will have someone build qualities and characteristics into your life from what he or she has learned and from which you will benefit. In a similar way, you will build into another person's life. Others in your life may be on the same or a similar level as you. These are peer groups, which generally consist of family and friends at different levels of relationship. Peer-mentoring or co-mentoring involves those people with whom we relate naturally because we have so many things already in common.

This model of accountability is a safeguard to help us walk closely with the Lord. Mentors will change occasionally, but they will each have the same clear and defined purpose in helping us to finish well.

Next Step

Let's revisit the questions from **Let's Get Started** as you complete this section.

Are you a better talker or listener? Or both?

_____

_____

For you to have a meaningful relationship/friendship with someone, what needs to take place?

_____

_____

Does a particular relationship cause strife or awkwardness in your life at this time?

_____

_____

Is the social networking model in your life working for the purposes you've intended?

_____

_____

1. Recognize your strengths and weaknesses in developing and/or maintaining friendships/relationships by sharing them below:

My strengths:

_____

_____

My weaknesses:

_____

_____

2. Considering your areas of weakness listed in question number one, note the following:

Problems I can solve if I choose to take action:

_____

_____

Problems I can't solve but will pray about:

_____

_____

3. Considering what you can solve, list several ways you can take action:

- _____

- _____

- _____

Fine-Tuning

Of the several ways you listed under **Next Step #3**, choose one that you will concentrate on specifically this week.

- _____

On Your Own

1. What is your desire/purpose in a friendship? Are you willing to make it a priority?

    _____

    _____

    _____

    List three people you would be willing to get to know better. Make time this week to have conversation with at least one you have listed. You may have to work it into your schedule. How will you do that?

    • _____

    • _____

    • _____

2. Study this list. See how many categories you can check off with a moderate amount of effort this coming week. Use the questions we wrote down in the Stop—Look—Listen section if you need help in starting conversation. This exercise can be quite fun!

☐ Below, write the names of those you've had at least a five to ten minute conversation with from the categories listed below:

☐ Someone with whom I work:

☐ Someone who is not a Christian:

☐ Someone with whom I have difficulty getting along (use initials or just a check mark):

☐ Someone in my neighborhood:

☐ Someone in my own church with whom I don't usually talk:

☐ Someone in my immediate family:

☐ Someone in my extended family:

☐ Someone born in another country:

☐ Someone in the junior-high age range (not in my family):

☐ Someone in the senior-high age range (not in my family):

☐ Someone over seventy years of age not related to me:

☐ My spouse:

☐ My children:

☐ Someone you have never met before; at the store, running an errand, etc. (use a check mark):

Summarize what you have learned from this exercise:

_____

_____

Write out and memorize Philippians 2:4:

_____

_____

_____

_____

SESSION EIGHT
THE WORKPLACE
AND THE HOME

Let's Get Started

1. Describe the work you do if you are employed (no matter how many hours) outside the home:

_____

_____

Do you find it satisfying? How would you rate your job satisfaction on a scale of one to ten, with ten being the highest?

_____

_____

2. Whether or not you are employed outside of the home, you will have work to do in the home. Describe what work you do there:

_____

_____

Do you find this work satisfying? On a scale of one to ten, with ten being the highest, rate your satisfaction:

_____

3. If you could choose any line of work, what would you choose to do?

_____

_____

4. Why do you work? What are your purposes?

_____

_____

Today's Topic

Since the fall of mankind, God intends that we work. Some of us love what we do, and others put their time in on the job, tolerating the work until the day is done. Some women who work outside the home often have a secret or not-so-secret desire to be a full-time homemaker. Many full-time homemakers would love the challenge or change that they feel a job outside the home might give them. Many men would love to retire early from what they are doing, and yet others spend fifty to seventy hours a week at their jobs. No matter what we do, the grass always seems greener on the other side. Both sides have advantages. We need to determine the best balance and primary purpose for ourselves.

No doubt, God can and does use Christians in any position in the workplace or in the home. Just as we learned the importance of relationships in our lives, we must learn to see how God wants us to fulfill his will in our lives and touch others through the work he has given us to do. We must individually determine through prayerful consideration where he wants to use us! No matter what our profession, God can use us. It's not so much what we do for a living but what we do with our lives.

As a mother at home with three young children, I must admit, I occasionally had difficulty determining where God was at work in my day. As a full-time homemaker, I felt I went from one tedious job to another until I collapsed in bed at the end of an eighteen-hour workday! Most days were a blur. And I remember a few that were so challenging that I really hoped I wouldn't wake up and have to do it all over again. But as I gave the struggles of my day to God, he showed me where the victories were. He also showed me where many of my errors and sins were—which was why I wasn't experiencing daily victories. I wasn't Spirit-filled.

At one point Joe and I realized why we had so many frustrations and so little free time. When we were newly married, we had each other. We were counseled to be cautious about having too many responsibilities (Deuteronomy 24:5) outside of our jobs and our marriage the first full year so that we had time to learn about each other. But then in addition to marriage, Joe's dental practice, and my teaching, we added ministry. We both loved everything we were doing, and we were able to do much of it together. We seemed to be building a strong relationship between us, and we were very happy. As time passed we kept adding to our lives: children, their activities, additional ministry, travel, friends, continued discipleship, my working at the office, and then adding doing the books at home. The list could go on! None of the things we were doing were wrong or sinful. What was wrong was that we only kept adding to our schedules, and we never seemed to think that we should cut out a few things or balance the things that were in our life. We realized we could not keep adding activities at an already busy time of life with small children, and live on fewer than six hours of sleep! Though well meaning, we found that this schedule was not conducive to life!

As a result of determining our purpose in life and setting goals, I believe we have been more content in our work, and better able to see how God works. Let me share a few things that helped us in the workplace and the home. I hope you will be able to apply some of what you will learn to your own life.

1. We desire to serve God both at work and at home. We want to be efficient and effective. To do that, sometimes we need to make changes. We take time to look at our involvement at work (and in all areas of our lives) and determine what really is right for our family and us. Because Joe was (and continues to be) self-employed, we may have made some work-related decisions differently from others who are employed by small companies or in the corporate world. We have made many decisions that we could not have made if we were not self-employed. One decision/ goal we made was that we did not want to continue working longer and harder as the practice grew and as the years passed.

   When Joe began his dental practice, he knew he had to work evenings and Saturdays in order to build a patient base, but as the years went on, it became increasingly difficult to be away from home and the children if we wanted to accomplish goals in the area of relationships. At some point he dropped one of his two evenings and decided to work every other Saturday. The practice continued growing, and Joe could have easily been at work eighty hours a week.

Instead, he decided to employ an associate so that the patients are able to continue getting dental care during the evening and nearly every Saturday. That allowed Joe to have time with family and not neglect his patients.

Because of our involvement in a number of ministries, our ultimate goal over the years has been to have Joe work less while maintaining the same income level. Thus, we are able to have time with family and friends, the ministry, etc., and continue to support financially the ministry work that we do. The raise doesn't come with bigger paychecks but in more time to be involved with what we have determined to be important in our life.

2. Whether I am helping Joe with his work or he is helping me at home, doing ministry together, or spending time with family or friends, we have purposed to work as a T.E.A.M. We are on the same side working together. That prevents many disagreements before they even start.

3. We agreed to teach our children the value of relationships and hard work. We recognized that if they (and we) watched hours of television, household chores, extracurricular activities, homework, and time spent with friends and family would not be the priority. We wanted our children to know the value and reward of both people and projects (work). To value work, they needed to realize that work is to be done; and when it is done, they will have time for other activities. We

needed to look for what would motivate each child. It worked like this: Whatever motivated the individual child became the "dangling carrot" for that child. If practicing their musical instrument/voice wasn't done, if laundry wasn't folded, if homework wasn't completed, they were not permitted to do other activities like visiting friends, attending sports events, going to youth group, shopping with friends, going to a movie, etc. Once we learned what motivated each child (i.e., the dangling carrot), they learned to accept the responsibility of getting their work done without our having to be the "bad guys." More will be discussed in session twelve on delegation.

One result we have seen of giving our children responsibilities is that they are unafraid of work and have learned that it can be fun. Many Saturdays the girls wanted to get up early and go to work with their dad! They have enjoyed learning to file, make bitewing X-rays, and greet patients. They also liked getting paid for their work! The various responsibilities at home and helping with ministry details helped them learn to serve and not always be served! Imagine if that idea caught on in our families, churches, neighborhoods, and workplaces!

4. We realize that we need good tools to do a good job at work. Whatever can help make our jobs run more efficiently and effectively—and if we can afford it— we should do. Using poor tools means we will have to work harder and use more energy. That usually

means we will deal with more frustration. Imagine if every time you used your stapler, you had to readjust the staples. You would waste time and energy and eventually you will become frustrated. Imagine if Joe used instruments that weren't in good condition. Both he and the patient would be frustrated! Read Ecclesiastes 10:10 for God's perspective.

5. Many jobs (filling teeth, washing dishes, doing homework, etc.) do not have a direct eternal purpose. Many jobs leave people feeling very insignificant. We must always find our significance, worth, and value through Christ. We are not adequate in ourselves, but our adequacy comes from God. Read 2 Corinthians 3:4–5. We always desire to find a way to relate what we do in a temporal setting to the value it could have in eternity. Joe has led people to Christ in the dental chair! (Of course, he has a captive audience!) And I had the assurance that no matter how tedious a job was at home, my goal was to raise the children in the ways of Lord. Both examples show an eternal perspective in a temporal setting. What would our jobs be like if we treated them like full-time ministry positions?

6. We desire to show appreciation and thankfulness as often as possible. Whether you are an employer or an employee, occasionally you will feel no one appreciates you or the job you do. If you give out bonuses, you may feel unappreciated when no one thanks you. But when we have been given something, do we

remember to show our thankfulness? When Jesus healed the ten lepers (Luke 17:11–19), only one of them showed his appreciation. No matter what others do or don't do, we want to be fair and even generous. For those working for others, it is important to be content with what you are paid (Luke 3:14).

One thing about work and time management goes hand in hand. We always seem to have or find the time to do it. If we work outside the home, we're expected to be there. If we work inside the home, not only are we expected to be there, but overtime is expected every day! No matter how we feel about work, we need to go. So what is there then to balance? What can we learn that will help us develop a well-balanced life? Read 1 Corinthians 15:58 for an exciting perspective.

> Work to live. Don't merely live to work.

Stop—Look—Listen

1. Read Genesis 1:26–30 and Genesis 2:15, 19. What was Adam's original job description?

_____

_____

Read Genesis 3:16–19. As a result of the fall (the disobedience of Adam and Eve), what did God say their job description would now be?

For Adam:

_____

For Eve:

_____

2. In 2 Thessalonians 3:10, what does scripture say about why we need to work? And what should the consequence be if we do not work?

_____

_____

Notice that scripture does not say "cannot" but "_____."

3. What is Jesus' purpose for us in our line of work? Read John 6:27 and summarize it in your own words:

_____

_____

What should our attitude be no matter what kind of work we are doing?

_____

_____

Read the following verses and put them into your own words:

Colossians 3:17

_____

_____

Colossians 3:23–25

_____

_____

Psalm 90:12, 17

_____

_____

Can you have this perspective at your place of work?
Explain:

_____

_____

4. What does God think about those who do not provide for their families? Read I Timothy 5:8. Discuss.

_____

_____

5. What does God want our ambition to be in our work and in our life? Read 1 Thessalonians 4:11–12.

_____

_____

6. Can we (should we) enjoy our work? Read Ecclesiastes 5:18–20. What will be the result of enjoying our work? (v. 20)

_____

_____

7. In order to believe we have "worth" or "significance" on the job, we must believe that it is God who has placed us there. Believing that to be true, we certainly should reflect Christ in our place of work. Speak to the following questions below as you consider what you are like "on the job":

_____

_____

Does how you work at your place of employment, at home, or at school set a good example?

_____

Does your family (both spouse and children) understand what your priorities are by the choices you make?

_____

Do those you work with or work around see Christ reflected in your life?

_____

Do you show what it is to be a Christian? How?

_____

How do you (and should you) handle criticism?

_____

Are you humble? Do you submit to authority?

_____

Are you a person of integrity? How do you show it?

_____

Do you pray for others at work? Are they aware of it?

_____

8. God created the universe in six days (Genesis 1:1–
    2:3, Leviticus 23:3; Exodus 20:9, 10) and rested on
    the seventh. Considering the work God did and that
    he rested, tell how important you think it is for you
    to rest one day out of the week? Do you?

_____

Next Step

1. Recognize the areas needing attention in order to
    balance or change your personal life in terms of the

work you do. If you can't think of any, ask your spouse or coworker!

- _____

- _____

- _____

- _____

2. Problems I can solve if I choose to take action:

_____

_____

_____

Problems I can't solve but will pray about:

_____

_____

_____

3. Considering what you can solve, list several ways you can take action:

- _____

- _____

- _____

Fine-Tuning

Of the several ways you listed under **Next Step #3**, choose one that you will concentrate on this week.

- _____

On Your Own

We are God's fellow workers. Whether on the job, at home, in school, or in ministry, we work with God. How exciting! Read 1 Corinthians 3:5–8. How can you relate these verses to your job and your ministry?

_____

_____

Write out and memorize Proverbs 16:3:

_____

_____

_____

If you would like to learn more about those who had a "mind to work," read Nehemiah's thirteen chapters. If you read two chapters a day, you will be finished within a week!

SESSION NINE
FINANCES

Let's Get Started

1. What is money?

_____

_____

2. If Jesus were to give you your heart's desire and you could ask Him for anything, what would you ask for?

_____

_____

3. If Jesus gave what you asked for in number two, what do you think it would do to your life? Would your life be changed in any way? Do you think you would be more or less content?

_____

_____

4. If you needed to "downscale" (buy less, save more, give up activities, etc.), would you be comfortable with the idea? Why or why not?

_____

_____

Today's Topic

Money and finances can be a tough topic because everyone has an opinion about it. Many times we have an opinion on how others use their money, but we must know our own views because God looks at our hearts to judge whether we are doing what we should with the resources he gave us. I love the topic because as a Christian, what we do with our money becomes a testimony. The wonderful thing about this testimony is that if we are faithful, good stewards (one who manages another's resources—in this case God's), God is glorified!

People say they value their teeth and yet don't want to spend the time and money to maintain them. Although Joe teaches preventative care to his patients, they may not adopt the right attitude, letting this important health discipline go. People always have time and money for what is important to them. Attitude and perspective are the determining factors in how we spend our money. Our attitude toward money will be reflected in all areas of our lives: priorities, family, health, our values, spending, and even God. For instance, when the children were young and had one ear infection after another, I hated spending the money to hear the doctor say, "Everything is clear." I guess I wanted to pay only if they had an infection! A number of situations caused me to be very thankful that there are good doctors that we can pay to provide the health care we need. How sad it would have been to not see a doctor and then deal with hearing loss or deafness as a result of a lack of proper care. It was all in my perspective and my attitude.

Some Christians believe *all* Christians should take a vow of poverty; however, being poor does not make one holy and being rich does not make one holy either! If it were not for those with moderate or great wealth who provide for ministers, missionaries, and parachurch ministers, what would happen to them? Could we commit to praying for those who have wealth to make godly decisions about their finances instead of talking about what they should or shouldn't be doing with their resources? Could we give thanks for those who are generous in giving to God's work? I believe it could be exciting if we would take on this attitude!

What we do with our money shows what is important to us (Matthew 6:21). Money can be used for selfish living or to enrich life. Money is never the problem. It is the love of money that is the problem (1 Timothy 6:10). Those who have wealth have a major responsibility. Read Psalm 62:10c.

How are we to balance our finances? I believe we have three choices. We can choose to live in one of the following ways:

Beyond Our Means
(In Debt)

Within Our Means
(Within Budget)

Below Our Means
(Money Left At End Of Month)

How are Christians to balance their finances? We must apply scriptural principles and not break God's rules concerning the use of money. We know that taking a stand on the issue of finances can be quite contrary to what the "world" is presently doing. What does God instruct us to do? As God's people we are told to do the following:

1. Seek first the kingdom of God—Matthew 6:33

2. Be content—Philippians 4:11–12

3. Serve with the best of our abilities with what he has given us—Colossians 3:17

Those three points apply regardless of any material or financial resources we may have. The bottom line is that God owns everything, and that must be the premise upon which we base our lives. Anything short of that is deception.

What about those who lack finances? We should first ask ourselves a few questions to see where we are and where God wants us. Do we have a need to learn to be content in any circumstance? (Hebrews 13:5) Do we need to learn a lesson about seeking God first? Do we need to learn a discipline? Is a "test" being given? Is more giving to be done? Is character being developed? Do we need to learn to be more creative in the use of money?

For those who experience stress over money because of too many financial responsibilities, I suggest reading one proverb from the book of Proverbs in the Bible each day. Record all the verses concerning money. Ask God what he wants you to learn from his Word. The assignment can be completed in one month (Proverbs has thirty-one chapters). As we record what we are learning, I believe the scripture will allow us to see just what balance we need in this area of our life.

We need to realize what money is for. Money is first and foremost to provide for our needs (Matthew 6:31; 1 Timothy 6:7–8; Philippians 4:19). Money is also a way that God shows his power and might (Malachi 3:10);

furthermore, it can also be used to give to others in need (2 Corinthians 8:3, 14–15; Deuteronomy 15:7–8).

What should we do with what we're given? If you're married, as husband and wife you must be a team. Whether single or married, God is your coach!

In the game of financial freedom, we must follow some basic rules or guidelines. Financial freedom, for the sake of our study, will be defined as getting out and staying out of debt (the obligation of owing money or services). Being debt free is the goal of financial freedom. Here are a few of the game rules:

Plan a budget. Write it out. Have a course of action (Proverbs 16:9). The hard part is that you must stick to it (2 Peter 1:6). A budget will help you determine what you have to spend, and on what. It seems at first like an awfully restrictive responsibility, but if you stick to it, you can reach financial freedom with your plan.

Get out and stay out of debt (Luke 16:13; Romans 13:8). Do so by balancing your accounts at the end of each month. You plan to reduce your debt to zero dollars by paying all your outstanding bills. You must develop a savings plan. If this is a difficult area for you to be disciplined, perhaps you need to find someone who will hold you accountable to what you want to accomplish. Because we cannot address every issue in this brief study, it would be wise for you to look into some of the many good books written by Christian financial counselors. They will help you address issues that are specific to you with biblically sound principles.

Pay cash only. That does not mean you cannot use a credit card. It simply means you must be able to pay the credit card off at the end of each month. As you make purchases, ask yourself the following questions:

> Am I making this purchase on impulse?
>
> Do I need this item?
>
> How much do I really want this item?
>
> How long will this item last?
>
> Is it within my budget?
>
> Have I spent time in prayer about it?

If you cannot answer these questions to your satisfaction when making a purchase, don't do it. Also remember that you may overlook some answers to the questions; for example, sale items purchased with a credit card that cannot be paid off at the end of the month are not really "sale" items by the time you add finance charges. If it is not worth the price or if it will not last long enough to fulfill your reasons for making the purchase, is it worth purchasing? These are all very important questions to consider.

Save regularly. On one hand, if you spend every penny you earn, nothing will be available to save. Savings needs to be planned for future use: unexpected repairs, car replacement, college for the children, retirement for you, etc. On the other hand, we are told not to hoard money. Hoarding is hidden accumulation. When we hoard, we never really plan to use it. The money just "looks" good as it accumulates. We have all read stories of people who have hoarded money or things. I remember reading a story of a woman who canned food and crocheted blankets. After her death, her home was being cleaned out. Stacks of blankets and thousands of canned goods were found. None of them could be used because they were damaged by mildew, having sat so long. I couldn't help but think of how many people might have been kept warm and fed well had she shared her abundance instead of hoarded it. Read Ecclesiastes 5:13.

My father had a second cousin named Leonard. Growing up during the Depression, Leonard learned from his parents that he should put his money away to be used for "another day" when it would be needed. At eighty-two years old, Leonard asked my father, who was his only living relative, to handle his financial affairs because his health was failing. My father agreed, thinking things would be fairly simple based upon how he lived. Was Dad in for a surprise! His cousin had well over a million dollars, yet he lived like a pauper (Proverbs 13:7).

When my parents prepared his house for sale, they found pots and pans so old and dirty they had to be thrown out. He had rolls of toilet paper stacked in closets. He seldom left his home. Television may have been his only form of entertainment. The sadness in this story is that he had financial means to do things for himself and others, and neither received the blessing. Perhaps the blessing is that he lived out his days comfortably in a nursing home and upon his death, the remainder of his estate went to a church that he had designated. He had so much money that even with the nursing home bills, he continued to accumulate great wealth. Was the hoarding worth it? Maybe we can't even be fair in asking that question, not knowing God's ultimate plan. But the question is one worth thinking for our own lives.

Tithe regularly. Read Deuteronomy 14:22. Tithing is such a great blessing! According to scripture, a tithe is 10 percent of your earnings; and an offering, gift, or contribution is whatever additional you give beyond your tithe. We have made it a point since we became Christians that we would tithe from the first of our earnings. Each month, before any check is written to pay a bill, checks are written to our local church and each missionary organization we support. We do not want to hope that we have enough money to tithe at the end of the month. It is handled first. We do not tithe to get something back from God, but we believe we have received and seen many blessings as a result of faithful tithing. We have learned that you cannot out-give God! He never desires to withhold from us. Why do we want to hold on to what we think is ours when it really all belongs to him, and he asks for only a tenth to be given to his work? He will bless abundantly! (Malachi 3:8–10, Proverbs 3:9) We should not be surprised if God blesses in such a way that we are able to give additionally. That additional giving, over the tithe is our offering. Are you willing to see if you might boost giving to 15 percent, 20 percent, or even more? When our "house is in order" financially… it is possible.

Set goals and be disciplined. Decide your needs and wants, writing them out as you do your plans and goals. Be willing to accept his will. Be prepared for him to say "no." If he says "no," he always has a reason even though we may be unable to see it or understand it. As you watch God work in your life through the area of finances, relate what he is teaching you to the way you discipline and love, give and bless, withhold, and require waiting of your own children. The correlations will be amazing!

Keep your priorities straight. God has a plan for you. If you are listening, he will tell you. He will not necessarily, however, tell you the plan he has for your neighbor! We learned early in our marriage that some decisions we would make might not be popular with other people even when we believed God gave us a specific direction. One year into our marriage (1980), my father offered us a one-year-old car for $3,300. It was originally over $15,000. We knew we would need a new (or another) car to replace Joe's. At the same time, we were saving for the purchase our first home. Weighing all of the factors, we decided that we could not buy a brand new car for the price we would be paying for this car. We had the cash available. Purchasing the car at this time would allow us no loan payments and no interest. We would, however, have to begin saving again for a home. After doing a few calculations, we decided that in the long run, we would come out ahead if we made the purchase at that point.

By the time we decided to make the purchase, my Dad decided to reduce the price to $2,200! There was a downside, however: unfavorable comments from people, many from within the church. It was a large car, so we heard comments about it being too big for our needs. It was a luxury car, so we heard that it wasn't appropriate for Christians to drive such a stylish vehicle. We never told anyone about the situation surrounding how we were able to purchase it until several years later when we sold the car for $2,500. The decision to buy the car had been a good one, but we had to be able to focus on how God provided it and what he would ultimately do through that transaction regardless of what others would say about our decision.

As a result of that decision and others like it, we have never had to take out a loan for a car. Was the amount of money that we paid worth it? Was it worth it to never pay any interest? We think so! We then decided to be disciplined to put a car payment in the bank every month even though we did not actually have a car payment. This allowed us to be able to buy our first new car later on down the road by paying cash. Because of how we handled that decision and our subsequent savings, we have not had to make a car payment. The decision was right for us.

Using the same basic principles, we were able to pay off our second home within about seven years. Transitioning from a first home with a mortgage interest rate of 17 percent (yes, those were the days of the early eighties) to our second home with a mortgage rate of 9.5 percent, we were able to use the additional monies to pay off the principal. Residing in that home for sixteen years, continuing to make monthly payments to a savings account allowed us to pay cash for our third home.

When our girls were between thirteen and eighteen years old, we wanted to teach them the value of the money we earned for them to spend. We gave them a modest (this will vary from family to family) budget for clothing. We saw how some (girls, particularly) could spend for clothing, so we wanted them to learn early to carefully use money. We told them we would provide for coats, one pair of school shoes, one pair of tennis shoes, "essentials" for gals, and a bathing suit each year. Homecoming or prom dresses: there was a certain amount we'd contribute, and if the dress was more expensive, they had to pay the difference. They had to buy their own clothing with the budget we'd give them. If they spent it all, they were done. If they had some left over, it was theirs for the next season for clothing.

I love watching them as grown-ups when we shop together and they evaluate each purchase that they are now paying for on their own, "So, do I *love* this or can I live without it?" Words repeated from days gone by!

When it was time for college, we did something for our two girls that has turned out to be a good thing for them and us. We saved enough money for each of them to attend a state school for four years. They know it's their money for college only. We have some rules which attach to this money—here are a few:

1. We manage it.

2. They have to maintain a certain GPA (is was realistic for them).

3. It's not for "extras" like alcohol, spring break (please!), travel, dining out at restaurants, etc.

4. It's for educational expenses only. If they decide on a five or six year plan, then they are on their own to pay for that. If they choose a private school, they will need some scholarships, a job, etc. to cover the difference.

If they finish well (made wise choices, kept their grades up, etc.), whatever money is left, is theirs. It is so much fun to watch how hard they work, how careful they are in spending (or not), and how they keep track of what is left in that account. Our first daughter, who went to a private college, lived at home after her first year, finished early, finished well, and married four days after her last day of school with a nice "chunk of change" to start her married life.

It won't surprise you that we used a similar method to pay for her wedding. When she and her wonderful fiancé Cosmin began planning their wedding, we told them that we were giving them a certain amount of money for a wedding gift. It was all theirs, but they were to use it as they wished for their wedding. We managed the bills as they came in, but the father and mother of the bride, as well as the bride and groom knew just what funds were available. Can you guess the ending? They planned a wedding within their budget.

It worked for us.

Not every financial decision we've ever made has been perfect or produced a great end result. The goal, however, is to have the right priorities and practice the principles that work over the course of time. Remember that many steps in the right direction get you where you want to go.

Putting God first will be reflected in the way you make financial decisions, apply God's Word to everyday life, use the resources of time, energy, money and talents that you've been given, and care for all he has given you.

> Keeping God first will allow us to see that he has provided everything needed for this very moment and for our contentment.

Stop—Look—Listen

1. What is money?

☐ A resource given by God

☐ A measure of success

☐ A testimony

☐ A savings tool

☐ A measure by which we ask whether or not we can afford something

☐ A spending tool

☐ The root of all evil

☐ A major area of discussion and arguments in marriage

☐ Fun if you have it

☐ Frustrating if you don't have it

☐ Evil if we have love for it

2. Read Matthew 6:25–34 and Philippians 4:19. Jesus would tell you not to be anxious about what kinds of things? Have you been anxious about how things would work out in a particular situation regarding finances, only to see the Lord work in a way that you never expected? Were you trusting or doubting during the process?

_____

_____

_____

_____

3. When you make a purchase, what questions do you ask yourself (or *should* you ask) before you purchase it? This can include large or small items.

☐ _____

☐ _____

☐ _____

4. If you have children, tell what your line of reasoning is when you tell them "no" to something. Do you see any similarities between how you are trying to teach them and how God may be teaching you when he says "no" to you? Do you always tell your children why you told them "no"? Does God always tell us?

_____

_____

_____

_____

5. It seems to be a trend in our society that we think we need to have or own whatever items we use. In other words, many of us would never consider asking to borrow something we need to use for a short time or just once. Neither would we think of lending some-

thing. Why do we have this mentality? Is it wrong to borrow? Is it wrong to lend? How should we handle it if others ask to borrow? Should we lend our things freely? Instead of lending "things," could you barter your craft, talent, or skill?

_____

_____

_____

_____

6. It's nice to have money to buy the things we need, but "things" are not the most important commodities in life. What things cannot be bought with money? (Proverbs 28:6; Proverbs 28:11).

_____

_____

_____

_____

> We shouldn't complain about what we don't have
> but be thankful we don't get what we deserve.

Next Step

1. Recognize areas that need some attention in regard to your money management:

   - _____

   - _____

   - _____

   - _____

   - _____

2. Problems I can solve if I choose to take action:

   _____

   _____

   _____

Problems I can't solve but will pray about.

_____

_____

_____

3. Considering what you can solve, list several ways you can take action:

    - _____

    - _____

    - _____

Fine-Tuning

Of the several ways you listed under **Next Step #3**, choose one that you will concentrate on this week:

    - _____

On Your Own

1. List specific resources in each category below that you and your family would be willing to lend, share, give, or barter. I have started you off with some ideas. What else might you and your family be able to do:

Money/Goods	Time/Energy/Talents/Skills/Services
Clothing	Teach computer skills
Food	Babysitting
Housing	Prayer

Check the boxes below that you feel you have accomplished. The ones *without check marks* represent what you can do soon or might consider doing in the future. Check them off at a later date as you do them.

☐ Get financial help (financial planner, church leader, etc.)

☐ Make extra payments on any existing loans

☐ Go without using credit cards for one month or more

☐ Consider disposing of credit cards if they are a problem for you

☐ Set a goal: I will pay off all credit cards by

_____

☐ Find free entertainment

☐ Don't frequent fast food restaurants

☐ Plan a budget

☐ Begin tithing

☐ Tithe regularly

- ☐ Establish a will
- ☐ Use my home for fellowship, etc.
- ☐ Plan a moderately priced vacation
- ☐ Establish a trust
- ☐ Send an anonymous gift to someone in need
- ☐ Reduce car expenses (carpool, buy different car, etc.)
- ☐ Go through your household and personal belongings, giving away what you haven't used in the last year
- ☐ Stick to your shopping list
- ☐ Help out at a food kitchen
- ☐ Invest extra money and donate the profits
- ☐ Set a goal to spend less in a particular area that is too high right now
- ☐ Gift giving: Think about creative "gifts" of time
- ☐ Buy groceries for someone in need and donate them anonymously! (Staples, not perishables.)
- ☐ Invite others to dinner
- ☐ _____
- ☐ _____
- ☐ _____

☐ _____

☐ _____

Now…. do it. There is no time like the present.

Write out and memorize Proverbs 22:1–2:

_____

_____

_____

_____

FINANCIAL PLANNING THOUGHTS AND WORDS OF WISDOM TOWARD FINANCIAL FREEDOM

True freedom begins by accepting scriptural restraints—1 Corinthians 7:22

Money is to be used for our needs—Matthew 6:31; 1 Timothy 6:8; Phil. 4:19

Transfer ownership of everything to God—Proverbs 8:18; Deuteronomy 8:16–18; Matthew 6:24; 1 Chronicles 29:12–14

Get out of debt; owe no one—Romans 13:8

Do not borrow for depreciating items, it presumes upon the future—Proverbs 22:7; James 4:13–17; Proverbs 27:1

Accept God's direction—Matthew 6:27–34

Practice patience and caution in every financial venture—Proverbs 3:13, 14, 19–21

Establish written plans and goals—Proverbs 27: 23–24

Commit those plans to the Lord—Proverbs 16:3

Seek good Christian counsel—Proverbs 19:20; Proverbs 11:14

Seek counsel from parents—Proverbs 23:22

Seek counsel from spouse—Ephesians 5:31; Proverbs 1:5

Learn to exhibit a gentle and quiet spirit—1 Peter 3:4

Develop a family savings plan—Proverbs 21:20

Help others—Romans 12:16; Philippians 2:3–5

No purchase is too large or too small to pray about—Ephesians 3:20

Pass on an inheritance which insures a godly and responsible heritage—Proverbs 13:22; Proverbs 20:21

Reduce or eliminate the use of credit—Proverbs 27:12

Before purchasing, give God an opportunity to provide the item—Psalm 37:7a

Refuse to cosign or lend; avoid surety—Proverbs 22:26; 20:16; 17:18

Learn to recognize and reject swindlers—Proverbs 2: 12, 16

Have contentment in a moderate lifestyle—Philippians 4:12; Ps. 17:15

Do not overindulge—Ecclesiastes 2: 10–11

Have sales resistance—impulse buying is the sure way to bondage—I John 2:16

Excel in your work—1 Peter 4:11; 2 Thessalonians 3:10

Give God tithes and offerings. Commit God's portion first. He returns and multiplies to those who give freely and without thought of profiting. Proverbs 3:9–10; 2 Corinthians 9:6; Malachi 3:8–10; Deuteronomy 14:22

Refuse get-rich quick
schemes—Proverbs
28:22; Proverbs 21:5

A good name is better than
riches—Proverbs 22:1–2

Know the difference
between:

Needs (God supplies)—1
Timothy 6:8; Matthew 6:32

Wants—Luke 3:13–14

Desires—1 John 2:15–16

SESSION TEN
HOSPITALITY

"Be hospitable to one another without complaint" (1 Peter 4:9).

Let's Get Started

1. Describe a time you were extended hospitality and what you enjoyed about it.

_____

_____

_____

2. When was the last time you invited others to your home for hospitality? Describe the reason, who was invited, what you did, and what you served.

_____

_____

_____

3. What do you expect to give/receive from hospitality?

_____

_____

_____

4. Do you believe you extend too much hospitality, just enough, or do you think you should do more? Tell why you answered the way you did. Do you believe you are balanced or off-balance in this area?

_____

_____

_____

Today's Topic

Some may think that hospitality is women's work, but I can assure you that men are needed for the job. Over the years Joe and I have developed a routine that has worked for us. Our routine assures that everything runs smoothly. The routine includes who answers the door, greets guests, gets beverages, makes introductions, serves food, cleans up, etc. It includes our whole family at times. We want it to be fun all the time.

Hospitality is not the same as entertaining.

Hospitality is

- giving to guests in a generous, friendly way
- treating guests with generosity
- meeting the needs of others
- motivated from the heart to do the above

Entertainment is

- to amuse
- to seek pleasure
- to be showy
- impressive
- motivated from the heart to do the above

On occasion I have been asked if you can do both. Motivationally, the answer is "no." In other ways, "yes." Let me explain. Some people (I am one of them) love fussing over the details of putting together an evening of hospitality. While some might wonder, Why does she fuss?, or Why does she do the extras? I say, I love doing it—for you to enjoy! I truly enjoy setting a beautiful table, serving a nice meal, and meeting the needs of my guests through conversation. Adding a game or two somewhere in the evening to spark conversation or add laughter is also pretty common! Although elements of amusement are involved, my true motivation is to meet the needs of my guests. On the other hand, I am equally comfortable ordering pizza or serving one of my easy and simple standard meals when there isn't the time to fuss, but the desire to get together is.

For some people, hospitality comes somewhat naturally. They enjoy it, thrive on it, love to plan, prepare, and even do the cleanup required to have guests in their homes. Others need to practice and nurture their skills. As an individual or together as a couple, the following are basic requirements needed to be successful at hospitality:

1. **A willing attitude** (1 Peter 4:9). You can tell an unwilling host a mile away. Visiting the home of an unwilling host is uncomfortable and awkward. Later, as you think more about it, it's embarrassing. For hospitality to be successful you need a willing attitude.

2. **Show poise and graciousness** (Philippians 2:4–5). Dignity of manner and having or showing kindness is essential. We want to treat others kindly and with respect; always keeping in mind to treat others the way you would like to be treated is helpful. It is after all the whole point of hospitality! Make your guests feel as welcomed and comfortable as you'd like to feel in someone else's home.

3. **Have a purpose.** I am one who can use almost any excuse or reason to have guests in my home. Some of my favorite reasons are to keep friendships going, meeting the needs of others, getting to know someone new, fellowship, celebrations, and of course, food and fun!

4. **Keep things simple.** Although I love to fuss over preparations, I also like to do things simply at times. I highly recommend keeping things simple, especially if you are new to hospitality and when children are involved. Trying to set a special table and serve special foods with a lot of little ones can cause frustration. Keep it simple and everyone will have fun.

5. **You must know or learn the art of conversation!** If you don't know how to engage in conversation with others, it really *is* easy to learn. *Others, not me, is the key!* That doesn't mean you can't or shouldn't talk about yourself or your life. It merely means you show interest in others and preferably ask about them first.

I've made a number of observations over the years. It is interesting to watch and listen to guests as they enter a function. What do they first say? What do they first do? You will learn several things within the first seconds of greeting them. One thing you will learn is what the most urgent topics are on their minds. Is it the bad weather, their rough day, that they are happy to see you, how you are doing, etc. Secondly, you will get a feel for their general personality. Are they quiet, shy, reserved, funny, loud, boisterous, friendly, genuine, etc.? As you make some quick assessments of what is on their minds and what their personalities are like, you take it from there in conversation. Ask them about themselves, what they enjoy, how *their* day was, etc. As you get better at the art of conversation, you will learn how to handle those important initial moments as you greet your guests. You will also need to learn how to steer conversations in other directions. Sometimes you will need to take center stage from a talker and redirect conversation so others have opportunity to speak. Other times you will need to bring quiet guests into the conversation.

Additional suggestions:

- **Don't fear silence.** It gives others a chance to think before they speak and quiet people a chance to talk.

- **Comment on what others say.** Don't correct them. "That's interesting" is usually easier to hear than, "You've got to be kidding me—I'd never do that."

- **Don't be sarcastic.** Some people don't know how to take sarcasm, so let them get to know you before you spring your great sense of humor on them!

- **Avoid uncomfortable or questionable topics, especially in group settings.** As we discussed earlier, you can't enter into this level of conversation until you've gained the trust and friendship needed to "go there."

- **Don't interrupt others.** Let them complete their thoughts.

- **Remember that a bore is one who talks to you about himself or herself, but a brilliant conversationalist is one who talks to you about yourself!**

- **Make introductions.** Don't take for granted that everyone knows one another simply because *you* know everyone. When I realize I have made that error, I immediately gather those I have forgotten to introduce and make sure they have an opportunity to meet everyone they do not know or to whom they have never been formally introduced. Perhaps think of and share a commonality you observe between the two you are introducing. Allow them a starting point to start conversation. Once they are conversing, you can do the same for other guests, allowing plenty of interaction.

  I can make conversation with almost anyone. One time, however, I was invited to a wedding shower where I knew only the bride-to-be. She had not arrived, so I knew no one. No one greeted me at the door. No one took initiative to greet or meet me throughout the first initial moments of walking in alone. I felt very awkward the whole time! I wondered, *Does anyone wonder who I am and whether I really was invited or belonged here?* It got funnier and funnier as I sat there. I didn't even know whom to thank when I left! I share this example because it was very uncomfortable for me, and I am not usually uncomfortable in new surroundings or in meeting new people. Imagine how one might feel if that is an area with which they have difficulty. It would be sheer torture! Make each of your guests comfortable by introducing them to others!

- **Have nametags available.** For any group of ten or more I suggest nametags, unless everyone knows each other well. Be creative. Have them write out or decorate their own nametags. Having them draw their favorite hobby under their name or writing a word that describes their personality helps others to identify and remember them. Nametags are essential for those meeting new people at rapid fire. It also helps you as the host or hostess to recall names when you (and you will) draw a complete blank on the name of someone you have known for years or is close to you!

- **Icebreakers are fun!** If you have a large group or quite a few faces new to your group, icebreakers are great ways to get conversations rolling! Play games that get everyone involved.

- **Know your limits!** If crowds are too difficult for you, enjoy smaller groups. If big meals are more than you can handle financially or emotionally, plan to serve something very simple or even consider a potluck, where everyone can help out! Or simply plan dessert and coffee.

- **Be a server.** Look after your guests, meet their needs, and make them feel comfortable. Hospitality doesn't always mean you're serving a meal, but you are always a servant to others.

- **Don't limit those you serve.** Do your own study in scripture to learn whom you can and should serve. Read Luke 14:13–14; Isaiah 58: 7, Hebrews 13:1–3; James 1:27. Don't just serve your friends. Open your heart and home to others outside your social circle. Someone once told me that she didn't invite others to her home unless she liked them. She was a guest in my home more than once when she told me that. You can imagine how I might have felt having *never* been invited over! However, there are some people that you should not invite. Read on to find out whom.

- **Do not invite some people.** Read 1 Corinthians 5:11, 1 Corinthians 15:33, and 2 Timothy 3:1–5.

- **Organize your time.** Plan ahead, plan ahead, plan ahead! (Use the Hospitality Planner—Appendix H.) It is frustrating to be a guest watching your host and/or hostess fussing over details that *could have* and *should have* been taken care of before guests arrived. If you state that dinner will be served at 6:30 p.m., let your guests know when they can arrive (example: between 6:00 and 6:30 p.m.), but that you will be serving dinner as close to 6:30 as possible. Knowing the dinner schedule ahead of time will allow guests to adjust their daily schedule if it differs from their usual dinnertime, or to accommodate health issues.

- **Practice.** It takes practice. Don't be discouraged if everything isn't perfect—*it never is!* And quite honestly, most guests will be thankful when everything isn't perfect!

Stop—Look—Listen

1. Hospitality is easiest when you keep your home at a point of maintenance at which things are generally straightened and cleaned up to allow the freedom to have company *any* time and for drop-in company to stop for a visit without its being a bother to you. By keeping your home at this point of maintenance, you will eliminate a number of excuses keeping you from opening your home for hospitality. List below as many excuses as you can think of that you may have said that keep you from opening your heart and home to guests. I'll list several to get your thoughts going, and you can add others!

☐ My home isn't decorated nicely enough.

☐ I can't afford it.

☐ I'm afraid I won't do a nice job.

☐ My house is always a mess.

- ☐ _____
- ☐ _____
- ☐ _____
- ☐ _____
- ☐ _____
- ☐ _____
- ☐ _____

Now read 1 Peter 4:9–10. Go back through the list above and check which reasons are valid reasons for *not* extending hospitality after reading the scripture verse.

2. Of the points you learned that are needed for having successful hospitality, which come easily to you?

_____

_____

_____

_____

_____

3. Of the points you learned that are needed for having successful hospitality, which are difficult for you? Do you know anyone who could help you develop success in those areas that are difficult for you?

_____

_____

_____

_____

_____

4. To those who provide a lot of hospitality but are seldom asked to receive hospitality, be encouraged. You will be blessed in other ways! Read Proverbs 11:25 and summarize it.

_____

_____

_____

_____

5. List some ways that you can show hospitality by meeting needs outside of your home. I have listed a few ideas to get you started:

- Taking a meal to a new mom or someone who just had surgery.

- Sending a note to someone—letting them know you are thinking of her or him. Read Proverbs 25:25.

- _____

- _____

- _____

Next Step

1. Recognize areas that need some attention in regard to balancing your hospitality opportunities and developing your hospitality skills and attitudes:

- _____

- _____

- _____

- _____

- _____

2. Problems I can solve if I choose to take action:

_____

_____

_____

Problems I can't solve but will pray about:

_____

_____

_____

3. Considering what you can change, list several ways you can take action:

- _____

- _____

- _____

Fine-Tuning

Of the several ways you listed under **Next Step #3**, choose one that you will concentrate on this week.

- _____

On Your Own

Within the next month, plan one "hospitality" opportunity in your home. Use the Hospitality Planner to help you plan and organize. Enjoy the planning, process, preparations, and your guests!

_____

_____

Write out and memorize 1 Peter 4:9:

_____

_____

_____

_____

SESSION ELEVEN
DELEGATION

Others will not do what is being done for them.

Let's Get Started

1. What jobs/chores do you do at home, work, or in the ministry that you would gladly give up if you could find someone else to do them?

_____

_____

_____

2. If you have children, list their names and ages and what jobs/chores they are responsible to do at home:

_____

_____

_____

_____

3. For what jobs were you responsible in your home while you were growing up? Put a check by the ones you didn't mind doing. Mark an "x" by the ones you never liked and still don't!

☐ _____

☐ _____

☐ _____

☐ _____

Today's Topic

Delegating is a wonderful way to distribute some of the work you have on your shoulders. Delegating takes practice. Some people are great at delegating. They delegate to you, and you don't even know it happened. It happens at work, in the home, in ministry, and on committees.

Sometimes the tasks we have in our lives become more than we can handle alone. Our lives are thrown out of balance because we have our own responsibilities *and* the responsibilities of others! Others may be capable of helping but not given an opportunity to take on a new responsibility in order to help lighten our load. Sometimes we have to be strong and courageous to "just say no!" If needed, reread Session One to refresh your memory on how, when, and why to say "no."

Teamwork, delegating, and cooperation are needed in business, at home, in ministry, in school, etc. I once read about the Tate family. Perhaps you've heard of them, too. Their story has been told via numerous websites. "The Tates pervade every organization. There is Dick Tate, who wants to run everything. Ro Tate tries to change everything. Agi Tate stirs up trouble whenever possible (and Irri Tate always lends a hand). Whenever new ideas are suggested, Hesi Tate and Vege Tate pour cold water on them, and Imi Tate tries to mimic everyone. Devas Tate loves to be disruptive. Poten Tate wants to be a big shot. But it's Cogi Tate, Medi Tate, and Facili Tate who always save the day and get everyone pulling together." They need to meet up with the "Gate" and "Brate" families and learn to delegate and celebrate!

Probably the best place to begin delegating, if you have children, is at home. Strong families will share or delegate chores and manage time together for everyone. Children need responsibility, and I believe they need it early. Responsibility gives them a sense of belonging and helps them develop positive self-esteem. Children in preschool learn sorting. They learn to put the blue round peg in the blue round hole. The application can easily be made at home. Forks and spoons fit into silverware trays. By practicing this skill at home, they learn the same tasks at home that they do at school: organizing, following directions, and learning shapes. Here are some of the tasks children can learn to do and what they will learn by doing them:

Age	Chore/Job	What They Will Learn
3	Set the table, fold small towels and rags, put silverware away (adults do knives)	Sorting, organization, following directions
4	Empty small wastebaskets, dress themselves, pick up their own toys, help you mix when cooking	A sense of belonging and responsibility to self
5	Earn money for chores or be given allowance, fold socks, undergarments, towels, and small simple items (not sheets, blankets, shirts) and be able to put them away where they belong	Value of money, greater independence, responsibility to self and family
6	Care for family pets, carry out garbage, help with recycling, replace/refill toilet paper and tissue containers	Caring for life, goal setting, meeting needs beyond self and family into community
7	Help pack or prepare lunches, answer phone and take message	Meal planning, attention to details, listening skills and telephone etiquette
8	Dust, basic baking and cooking with help, scheduling schoolwork projects	Measuring, reading, meal preparation, goal-setting and following through with assignments
9-12	Laundry (washing and drying), vacuum, bathrooms, observe paying of bills	Reading, measuring, organizing, prioritizing, paying bills on time, balancing accounts

Add responsibilities according to the abilities and ages of your children. All chores need to be taught first. If they aren't done properly or with the right attitude, help them until they can do it on their own. You must be their example. Always give encouragement and tell them you are thankful so they do not become frustrated. Your goal should be your child's independence at age eighteen.

How much time they spend doing chores will depend on how much they have to do and how you want it done. As you watch your children take on these household responsibilities, you will gain additional time, and they will learn many skills they need to get along in life. Whether you need to implement delegating at home, at the office, or in ministry, a few things will help you accomplish it. Let's take a look at a few biblical examples.

Moses learned to delegate after his father-in-law Jethro observed the hours he (Moses) was keeping. Jethro recognized that Moses was out of balance, and told him it was not good. He explained that the task was too much for Moses and that he and the people would become worn out. He told Moses that he could not do this alone. He broke down the responsibilities that Moses had and told him to select able men who feared God and place them over different groups of people. By sharing authority and empowering others, the legal system would be more efficient and the people would go away satisfied. Probably the most significant point in this example, besides the advice Jethro gave, was that Moses *followed through* on all his father-in-law recommended! Read Exodus 18:13–27 to get the full picture.

God the Father delegated duties to Jesus in Matthew 11:27. In each account of Jesus feeding the four thousand and five thousand, he delegated to those around him to give him the fish and loaves, to serve them, and then to bring him what was left (Mark 6:35–44; Matthew 15:32–38). Jesus delegated watching and praying to Peter, James, and John (Mark 14:32–42). Jesus gave his disciples the job and the authority to cast out unclean spirits, heal sickness and diseases, to preach, raise the dead, cleanse the lepers (Matthew 10:1–8). And we can delegate things over to him! (Matthew 11:28–30) We can see delegation in what God entrusted to Jesus, Jesus to his disciples, the disciples to us, and we to disciple others. The command and delegation is given in Matthew 28:18–20. Delegation is seen throughout scripture. We must learn how and when to use it based upon our work, ministry, family load, and responsibilities. We have wonderful examples. Let's be faithful to implement what we've learned.

Here are some ideas that will help you to successfully accomplish delegating. It will take practice.

- *Ask* others which responsibilities and duties they would like to assume. A new job can sometimes be more appealing than one you've had forever. By asking what others would like to do, you may find that people will joyfully use their talents and gifts!

- *Show* others their new responsibilities. You cannot expect a job to be done well if the individual has never seen it done or done it. Give her or him time to watch you or one who can clearly demonstrate the task. Provide the opportunity to ask questions. Then the person can be sure to understand what is expected. Give the person time to show you how she or he does the task so that you can help make needed changes to do a good job. Thoughtful delegation will save you the frustrating experience of trying to put square pegs into round holes.

- *List* whatever steps need to be accomplished. Seeing it written is helpful until it becomes a habit. This may mean writing a job description. Failing to communicate clearly leads to many unhappy people and problems.

- *Lower Your Standards* when giving up a job that you have done for a long time. It is not likely to be done with the same swiftness or thoroughness that you were able to do it. You may need to lower your standards as you teach and train. Increase your standards as you see progress. Complete delegation occurs when you can delegate something to someone and entrust to them full authority for that responsibility as well. Paul entrusted Timothy with authority and responsibility (1 Corinthians 4:15–17).

- *Switch Roles* occasionally. Sometimes trading a job can be an appealing way to get a fresh new outlook on work.

- *Do Jobs Together* at home, at work, and in ministry. Working together is sometimes more fun than working alone. In addition, work gets done more quickly!

- *Form a Committee* that will help assign and delegate jobs. Be sure to choose the right person for the right job and hold her or him accountable for how the task is fulfilled and accomplished.

- *Encourage* others with words of sincere encouragement and praise. People will generally give more and stay at a job longer if they are rewarded with kind words.

- *Expect the Best* and hopefully you will see the fruit of your hard work and theirs.

The above list can be discussed with regard to the family, the work environment, the ministry area, the classroom, etc.

Stop—Look—Listen

1. Under **Let's Get Started** question number one, you listed jobs/chores you would gladly give up if you could. What would it take for you to delegate at least one of those listed?

_____

_____

_____

_____

2. Under **Let's Get Started** question number two, you listed your children and what chores they do. Do you feel they do enough/not enough based upon age appropriateness of chores?

_____

_____

_____

_____

3. What creative ways can you think of to redistribute chores in your home? At work? In ministry?

_____

_____

_____

_____

4. When you "give up" a job and delegate it, do you ever want to take it back? Why?

_____

_____

_____

_____

5. Read Exodus 18:13–27. Why didn't Moses think of
   Jethro's plan of action by himself?

   _____

   _____

   _____

   _____

6. What specific chores/duties/work can you assign to
   others to free yourself up to do that which only you
   can do?

   _____

   _____

   _____

   _____

Next Step

1. Recognize areas that need some attention in regard to how and why you need to delegate:

   - _____

   - _____

   - _____

   - _____

   - _____

2. Problems I can solve if I choose to take action:

   _____

   _____

   _____

   Problems I can't solve but will pray about:

   _____

   _____

   _____

3. Considering what you can change, list several ways you can take action:

- _____

- _____

- _____

Fine-Tuning

Of the several ways you listed under **Next Step #3**, choose one that you will concentrate on this week.

- _____

On Your Own

Write out the key points of how delegation was accomplished in these verses:

Exodus 18:13–27

_____

_____

_____

Matthew 11:27

_____

_____

_____

Matthew 10:1, 5–14

_____

_____

_____

Matthew 28:18–20

_____

_____

_____

What is your responsibility, as you see it, regarding balancing your life through delegating?

_____

_____

_____

Write out and memorize Colossians 3:23:

_____

_____

_____

_____

SESSION TWELVE
REST—RELAXATION—
REFRESHMENT—FUN

Let's Get Started

1. What do you find relaxing and restful?

    _____

    _____

    _____

2. If you are married, do you and your spouse rest, relax, and refresh yourselves in the same way or differently?

    _____

_____

_____

3. Do you rest and relax often enough? How often is often enough for you?

_____

_____

_____

4. Do you find what you do for rest and relaxation helps you to be refreshed?

_____

_____

_____

Today's Topic

If you are the playful, fun-loving type, you will wonder why we even needed this session. You are a party waiting to happen, and you are "happening" all the time! If you are the hard-working, driven-to-perfection type, you probably wish we had done this session a long time ago. You needed to balance your active and busy life before today! No matter what our tendencies, we all need rest and relaxation to be refreshed. A joyful heart and laughter is something that helps us as we have fun in life as well! (Ecclesiastes 3:4, Proverbs 17:22)

You can find many scriptural examples of people taking and making the time to rest. We'll look at just a few of them, but as you read scripture, take note of different people who are recorded as having taken the time to rest. Let's start with God! After creating the heavens, the earth, light for night and day, plants, trees, stars, birds, sea creatures, cattle, creeping things, etc., God took the entire seventh day to rest! (Genesis 1–2:3). If you read Exodus 31:17, you'll realize that he was recorded as being *refreshed!*

Sleep is rest. Most of us, according to the National Sleep Foundation, do not get enough rest and because of our lack of sleep, there are increased motor vehicle accidents, greater risk of diabetes, heart disease, and depression, the inability to pay attention, react to signals, or remember new information. NSF reports that most adults sleep less than seven hours per night, yet the average amount needed is between seven and nine hours.

How Much Sleep Do You Really Need?	
Age	Sleep Needs
Newborns (0-2 months)	12-18 hours
Infants (3 to 11 months)	14 to 15 hours
Toddlers (1-3 years)	12 to 14 hours
Preschoolers (3-5 years)	11 to 13 hours
School-age children (5-10 years)	10 to 11 hours
Teens (10-17)	8.5-9.25 hours
Adults	7-9 hours
	Source: National Sleep Foundation

In addition to sleep, we want to incorporate into the balance of life, times of prayer, relaxation, refreshment, and fun. Jesus was a guest at a wedding. He probably had a wonderful refreshing time! (John 2:1–11). He also took time to rest from performing miracles and being pressed by the crowds. He went alone to pray (Luke 5:16; 6:12, Matthew 14:23; Mark 1:35) and did that often! Sometime it was in the early morning, and other times it was late at night or through the night.

Taking time to pray is a great pressure and stressor reducer! Do we take the time we *need* to quietly wait on the Lord for answers to our prayers? Isaiah 40:31 says, "Those who wait for the Lord will gain new strength; they will mount up with wings like eagles, they will run and not get tired, they will walk and not become weary." Trusting in God's Word and reading this verse should interest and excite us as we wait to see how God will work that out in our lives!

When you feel the pressures of life overwhelming you, do you know when to stop? Sometimes we keep going, thinking we're fine when we aren't. A number of years ago, we experienced a challenging time of life. Daily we cared for all of our son Joey's needs (including showering, toileting, etc.), Joe's dad developed cancer and died seven months later, my brother took his own life, my own father was already in the middle of his six year downhill trend which included three very intense years of caring for him through Alzheimer's. At the end of those six years for Dad, my mom, the well parent, died of a massive heart attack, Dad following five days later. Should I be surprised that what followed was a seven week "stay in bed" back injury? Once up and functioning, we were in the midst of Kristina's high school graduation, college search, Joey's high school graduation and job search, when Joe's mom began needing care (including her showering and other needs), having been diagnosed with advanced vascular dementia. Add Joey's transportation needs of ten hours per week ... while continuing in the various ministries and Joe's work at the office. I began looking for a wig to cover the large fist-sized balding spot that appeared on the side of my head. I share this because I actually thought I was "handling things well." In reality I had not taken ample opportunity to actually process all that happened. I never really caught my breath from one crisis to another. I had to stop everything and regroup. I began clearing my schedule. I took meetings off the calendar. I expressed to family, friends, and ministry partners that

I needed to make some drastic changes. I began resting, and sleeping, and relaxing. Everyone understood.

How much better life could be if we could begin to recognize the stressors we face and balance them with rest or relaxation? After a day at the computer writing, I've learned I need to take a brisk walk. After a day watching a grandchild, I need an evening that allows me to kick my feet up and read a book or watch television. When I'm stressed because a big project is taking all of my attention, I focus down the road and plan a good time of rest or vacation that will balance that stress.

Sometimes the balance of our life tilts dramatically to one side because we have said yes to the wrong things. We say yes because we feel guilty, are afraid, seek approval, want a pat on the back, want more pay, want to be noticed, or are manipulated for someone else to get their way. We need to ask ourselves if we are saying yes because we feel we have to or because we are choosing to, based on our life circumstances and balance. (See Balancing the Active Life Questions—Appendix E to answer this question for yourself.)

At some time or another, to some degree or another, we will all sense the pressure and stress of the world around us. It's like driving on the highway. You know the speed limit is sixty miles per hour, but when everyone around you is passing you up at sixty-five to seventy miles per hour, it's easy to find yourself going with the flow! We have all done it. But when we realize we're over the speed limit, we must take action and get our foot off the gas pedal! If we continue in the fast lane, we could be headed for destruction! Whether a flat tire or an accident…we're stopped. Life is just like that. We don't realize what we are doing! We keep adding to our schedules. We allow ourselves to speed like those around us. We need to take action and reevaluate! We need to simplify; get a new perspective; try a new strategy; limit involvements. We need to pace our days and get daily rest and do the same with our weeks, month, and year. That could mean anything from a daily nap or reading a book for an hour, to planning that yearly vacation. Let's take just a few moments to do that now. And then—let's get serious about putting some relaxation and rest into our lives to allow ourselves the wonderful feeling that comes from being refreshed!

Stop—Look—Listen

1. Rest is sometimes a hard thing to do, let alone for which to plan! For many it must become a discipline. Read the following verses and summarize what God's Word is saying to you about rest:

    Psalm 37:7a

    _____

    _____

    _____

Proverbs 14:33a

_____

_____

_____

Matthew 11:28–30

_____

_____

_____

Mark 6:31

_____

_____

_____

Ecclesiastes 3:4; Proverbs 17:22

_____

_____

How do you *know* you are refreshed? List as many things that come to your mind that indicate you are refreshed:

_____

_____

2. Do you feel good when you are refreshed? Describe your mood (emotionally), how your body feels (physically), how your spirit feels (spiritually).

_____

_____

_____

3. Are there times you purposely choose not to rest? Why? Is it usually worth it?

_____

_____

_____

Next Step

1. Recognize areas that need some attention in regard to how you rest and relax:

    - _____

    - _____

    - _____

    - _____

    - _____

2. Problems I can solve if I choose to take action:

    _____

    _____

    _____

    Problems I can't solve but will pray about:

    _____

    _____

    _____

3. Considering what you can change, list several ways you can take action:

- _____

- _____

- _____

Fine-Tuning

Of the several ways you listed under **Next Step #3**, choose one that you will concentrate on this week.

- _____

On Your Own

We know there is a need to provide our bodies the rest and relaxation they need. But will we actually *do* it?

Look back over **Let's Get Started** number one. I have purposely kept this lesson short so there would be *"time"* to take the opportunity to do something you put on that list! What will you do?

_____

Go to it!

Share what you did to find rest, relaxation, and refreshment, and if you feel you accomplished what you set out to do!

_____

_____

_____

Write out and memorize Psalm 37:7a.

_____

_____

_____

_____

SESSION THIRTEEN
MINISTRY AND COMMUNITY

Let's Get Started

1. How do you serve/minister to the body of believers? List every way that comes to your mind:

   - ☐ _____
   - ☐ _____
   - ☐ _____
   - ☐ _____

2. How do you serve/minister to your neighbors, in your schools, through sports activities, in your community? List every way you can think of:

   - ☐ _____

☐ _____

☐ _____

☐ _____

After you have made your list, put a check in the box if you purpose in your heart to serve in a way that shows the love of Christ to unbelievers as opposed to primarily social involvement.

_____

3. Who is the first person who comes to your mind when you think of one who serves? In what ways have they served and what have you observed about their service?

_____

_____

_____

Today's Topic

We talked about relationships in **Session Seven**. You might find a review of that session helpful as you minister and serve not only within churches but also as you work out in the community. You will find so many needs everywhere and so many opportunities to serve and to share Christ with others. I hope this session will encourage you to be that messenger of hope to others!

No matter what you think you want to do, no matter what you hope or desire to do, no matter how much training you have, you will not have success unless you are committed!

Committed to:

- Jesus Christ as Lord and Savior of *every* part of you (body, soul, spirit)—Read Romans 6:6; John 14:27; Romans 12:2.

- Daily quiet time of reading in God's Word, the Bible, and prayer to determine his will for YOU! Read Psalm 1.

- Availability at all times, whatever the cost.

Each of us is motivated to do *certain* tasks. Some people are motivated to serve themselves. They want life to be convenient, easy, fun, and comfortable. They don't want their boat rocked. They don't want to extend their arms to serve, and overextending wouldn't even occur to them (unless, of course, they needed something for themselves and were looking for who might help them). The sad thing is that many Christians are like this! They fill many seats in churches. Church attendance makes them look good. Saying a little something spiritual looks good. Serving on a rare occasion looks even better. Their world is pretty small because it revolves around just one person—themselves! If you sense some conviction as you read this please consider *why* my comments may ruffle your feathers. After all, I don't know your heart—my comments are general and not aimed at any one person, and you are not accountable to me but to God. You don't have to justify your actions to me or take it up with me, but with Him!

It's okay to have your feathers ruffled. Just be sure you know to *whom* to respond! A number of years ago, I was the women's leader in our church for a large event being brought to Cleveland. My job description was to motivate women to come to the different preliminarily activities and ultimately help out in whatever way the Lord might lead them. On one particular occasion, I was to do a three minute "come and join us" talk to the whole church, which was directed to the women. I had prepared the three minute talk to encourage and enlist women to do whatever God called them to do to help in the church and in the community regarding this event. Many who responded found various ways to serve using their gifts, talents, and availability.

The very next day, I received a phone call from a very upset woman. I was thankful to have had the spiritual presence of mind to ask her if we could pray before we talked. She agreed. I prayed and asked the Lord to watch over our time together and our conversation. As soon as I said, "Amen," she screamed and cried. I won't restate the whole conversation, but it was pretty vicious. She basically wanted to tell me why she couldn't help and how I had no right to make people feel guilty about not helping. At the end of an hour of listening to her, I finally said, "I really need to go. I am sorry you see my 'call to action' as hurtful to you. You are obviously very angry, but as I looked over the congregation, I must tell you that I do not remember even seeing you. I did not know you were there, so please understand that nothing was directly spoken to you. Your anger isn't with me, but you are misdirecting towards me. I believe you need to speak with the Lord and see what he might be trying to say to you." She needed to be directed to the source of her conviction.

Others are motivated to do things not for self, but for God. They listen to his prompting even if the timing isn't always convenient, comfortable, easy or fun, because they see the bigger picture. Their world is big because they see the big picture involving more than just themselves. It involves God's plan! The picture isn't "my will" but "Thy will." The picture isn't just one small piece of the puzzle but all of the pieces connected together! This person realizes they are but one small piece and without them, the picture cannot be complete!

Which are you? Which one do you want to be? Which one will you choose to be? It *is* a choice. God will not force you to do anything. He will not force you to miss his blessings—he leaves that up to you.

I have often asked myself this question of well-known Christians, "What if _____ said, 'Lord, that sounds like a great idea, but not for me!'" Considering some of the great leaders in history and of our day, and their accomplishments in the sphere of Christianity, imagine if they had said those words! But because of obedience, which certainly came with a price, God was able to use them to share his word, point others to Christ, and many have learned and grown in the ways of the Lord.

None of us knows where our obedience to God will take us. We only know the next step. Will you be obedient to the next step? Wherever you are in your walk with the Lord, he will use you! Are you willing? Are you willing to give up your agenda for his? Are you willing to use the gifts, money, talents, and resources he has given you for Him? (Read Romans 12:3–9.) If you use the gifts he has given you as he has intended for them to be used, you will not be overloaded or burned out! He will energize you when you use it. We do not get overloaded from doing "too much." We get overloaded from doing "too much of nothing." When we are out of his will, not filled with his Spirit, we are out of balance with life. That is when we crash and burn.

If you have a ministry that originates from God in your heart and you are faithful to his call, then it will grow and you will see fruit! (Romans 7:4; Matthew 7:17–20). As your ministry brings forth fruit, you will see it reproduce beyond your church community into your neighborhood community! Outreach will become a natural part of who you are!

Whenever I am out of the church setting—with neighbors, volunteering in the schools, at civic events, etc.—I always say one thing that I hope will make the person I am talking to aware of my relationship with Christ. My comment may be that I'm praying about something, or if they have shared something with me that they are having difficulty with, I say I will pray for them. They may mark me as "religious," but I take it as a great start! If they don't learn about the need for God from me, who will they hear it from? If I wait for a long time before saying something about the Lord, it gets harder and harder to bring up conversations later that are of a spiritual nature. It allows me an open door to someday tell about the most wonderful thing that has ever happened in my life—coming to know Jesus as my Savior.

If we never speak to others about our families in conversation, we might never tell others that we have a spouse and children. Imagine how awkward that would be! People would think we didn't care about our families. Do others realize and recognize that you know and love the Lord?

Enjoy sharing Christ with all those you meet! Enjoy the opportunities He puts before you!

> Faithfulness is God's requirement—
> Fruitfulness is God's reward.

Stop—Look—Listen

1. Read Ephesians 1:18–23. Specifically in verse 22, what is the position of our Lord Jesus Christ?

2.   Read Romans 12. Verses 6–8 give you a list of spiritual gifts. List them below and circle the gift with which you believe the Lord has gifted you.

_____

_____

_____

According to verses 9–21 how should we as Christians behave?

_____

_____

If we behaved like this in our churches and in our community, how would things be different from the way they are now?

_____

_____

_____

3. If Christ is the head (Ephesians 1:22) and we are the members, what happens if we don't do what the head tell us to do?

_____

_____

_____

4. All Christians are not gifted in the same way or asked to do the same things. We shouldn't feel that we should all do the same things, and we must be cautious to not judge others just because they aren't doing what we are doing. Christ is the head and commands the members to do what they should do. They must respond. Read John 4: 35–38. Explain how we are used of God as we respond to His call.

Must we think the job of ministry is for pastors only?

_____

_____

Must we think the job of ministry is ours alone?

_____

He calls us to work together to accomplish his overall "big picture"!

5. Read 2 Corinthians 6:1–10. In verse 1 who are we working with?

_____

In order that the ministry not be discredited, what must we do and under what conditions?

_____

Next Step

1. Recognize areas needing attention in regard to balancing your service in ministry and your outreach to the community:

- _____

- _____

- _____

- _____

- _____

2. Problems I can solve if I choose to take action:

_____

_____

_____

Problems I can't solve but will pray about:

_____

_____

_____

3. Considering what you can solve, list several ways you can take action:

- _____

- _____

- _____

- _____

- _____

Fine-Tuning

Of the several ways you listed under **Next Step #3**, choose one that you will concentrate on this week.

• _____

On Your Own

There is no end to the needs that are in our churches and individual communities. We can get very worn out or burned out if we misuse our gifts or misunderstand what he's asking us to do. It's easy to want to give up, and many do. Read Galatians 6:7–10. How can you apply these verses to your own life?

_____

_____

_____

Write out and memorize Galatians 6:9:

_____

_____

_____

_____

CONCLUSION

We began our study by laying a foundation based upon where each of us was. Our foundation, of course, is our relationship with our Lord. We can choose to continue in our own ways or in the ways of Jesus. That will only be accomplished, however, as we grow closer to him. Growing closer involves study in his Word, prayer, surrendering our own agenda and will, learning to listen, and obeying so that balance is indeed achievable. When we get to that point, we are able to set goals as we see where God works in and around us. We will see the evidence in relationships, at our work, in our home, in our finances, through our hospitality and fellowship, in our ministry, and in the community. Through these avenues God builds our character and faith in such a way that others are also drawn to develop lifestyles of commitment to God and balance that is appropriate for their callings in life. Only God can cause all of this to happen. To leave him out of any of these areas is to say that we don't need him. We know that nothing is hidden from God (Hebrews 4:13), so we must allow him access to our lives.

When we say, "This hasn't worked," we might just say, "I haven't really listened to God to let him teach me the solution." The most wonderful thing about a personal relationship with Jesus is that he will tell me what I need to learn, and he will tell you what *you* need to learn and how we should respond (Psalm 138:8). If our response is obedience, we will see results. If our response is disobedience and outward rebellion (demanding our own way and doing everything we can to get it; opposing any control of authority including God's), we will head for destruction and set an inappropriate example for those around us. I found it very interesting that the word following rebellious in my dictionary is the word rebirth! That is exactly what is needed for each of us! We need to be born of God in a rebirth that produces new life in us!

We need the faith that God will work in and through us. In Proverbs 24:10 we learn that if we don't have what we need in a time of crisis, we won't have the strength or the resources to handle it. We become unbalanced.

God has shown us that a false balance is not good (Proverbs 20:10, 23; Proverbs 11:1) and is an abomination, but he delights in a balance that is weighted justly.

You have been taught many things from the Word of God in these thirteen sessions. You are now without excuse. You must choose how you will implement each principle into your own life. We are all like the Israelites in the wilderness. We must choose obedience or disobedience. Let us not harden our hearts to the "promised land" that he has for each of us. There we will find purpose, see our goals through reached and rest (Psalm 95:6–11).

God has prepared us for the battles we will encounter, but let us remember that the *victory* is his! (Proverbs 21:31)

Now, whatever God asks you to do, wherever God asks you to serve, however God asks you to give, whatever God asks you to balance.....

do it now!

APPENDIX A
SOMETHING TO THINK ABOUT

Satan called a worldwide convention. In his opening address to his evil angels, he said, "We can't keep the Christians from going to church. We can't keep them from reading their Bibles and knowing the truth. We can't even keep them from conservative values. But we can do something else. We can keep them from forming an intimate, abiding experience in Christ. If they gain that connection with Jesus, our power over them is broken. So let them go to church, let them have their conservative lifestyles, but steal their time so they can't gain that experience in Jesus Christ. This is what I want you to do, angels: distract them from gaining hold of their Savior and maintaining that vital connection throughout their day!"

"How shall we do this?" shouted his angels.

"Keep them busy in the nonessentials of life and invent unnumbered schemes to occupy their minds," he answered.

"Tempt them to spend, spend, spend, then borrow, borrow, borrow. Convince the wives to go to work and husbands to work six or seven days a week, ten to twelve hours a day, so they can afford their lifestyles. Keep them from spending time with their children. As their family fragments, soon their homes will offer no escape from the pressures of work.

"Overstimulate their minds so that they cannot hear that still, small voice. Entice them to play the radio or cassette player whenever they drive, to keep the TV, the VCR, and their CDs (DVD's, MP3's, iPods, and....) going constantly in their homes. And see to it that every store and restaurant in the world plays music constantly. This will jam their minds and break that union with Christ. Fill their coffee tables with magazines and newspapers. Pound their minds with the news twenty-four hours a day. Invade their driving moments with billboards. Flood their mailboxes with junk mail, sweepstakes, mail-order catalogues and every kind of newsletter and promotional offering free products, services, and false hopes.

"Even in their recreation, let them be excessive. Have them return from their recreation exhausted, disquieted, and unprepared for the coming week. Don't let them go out in nature. Send them to amusement parks, sporting events, concerts, and movies instead. And when they meet for spiritual fellowship, involve them in gossip and small talk so that they leave with troubled consciences and unsettled emotion. Let them be involved in soul-winning. But crowd their lives with so many good causes that they have no time to seek power from Christ. Soon they will be working in their own strength, sacrificing their health and family unity for the good of the cause."

It was quite a convention in the end. And the evil angels went eagerly to their assignments, causing Christians everywhere to get busy, busy, busy, and rush here and there.

Has the devil been successful at his scheme?
You be the judge.

Author Unknown

APPENDIX B
HOW TO HAVE A
RELATIONSHIP WITH GOD

Many believe it is impossible to know the God of the universe. Having a relationship with God, because he is so awesome, holy, and pure can seem like an unattainable possibility, but the truth is this: the gospel—the teachings of Christ—and getting to know him are really quite simple. So simple, that some choose to complicate the message and truth and not believe in God, thinking they have something more to do than what Christ has already done for them. Follow along with me, as we discover who God is and what he has done—for you and for me.

While God reigns over the entire universe, he also cares about us in such a way that his love is evident in the plans he has for each of us.

"The Lord will accomplish what concerns me; Thy loving-kindness, O Lord, is everlasting" (Psalms 138:8).

"For God so loved the world that he gave his only begotten Son, that whoever believes in him should not perish but have eternal life" (John 3:16).

"I came that they (everyone) might have life, and might have it abundantly" (John 10:10).

We don't always recognize God's love for us because of our own sin (wanting our own way). That stubbornness will keep us separated from this loving and holy God. We can try all we want, even doing things we think will "earn" our way to pleasing God and ultimately thinking we can get into heaven because of good deeds. But because of our sin, we can't. We don't have the means to approach a loving and holy God because of our ugly sin. Our sin isolates and alienates us from him.

"All have sinned and fall short of the glory of God" (Romans 3:23). "All" means each of us.

"The wages of sin is death" (Romans 6:23).

Because of God's tremendous love for us he provided a way (through Jesus Christ) for every individual to know, trust and serve God. He died for our sin so we didn't have to.

"God demonstrates his own love toward us, in that while we were yet sinners, Christ died for us" (Romans 5:8).

"Christ died for our sins … he was buried … he was raised on the third day, according to the Scriptures. He appeared to Peter, then to the twelve. After that He appeared to more than five hundred" (1 Corinthians 15:3-6).

"Jesus said to him, 'I am the way, and the truth, and the life; no one comes to the Father but through Me'" (John 14:6).

This leads to the hardest and easiest of decisions; hardest because God asks us to individually choose whether or not we want to follow his way and receive his love through the provision of Jesus Christ—and easiest because he did everything for us. It's so simple it can be difficult to wrap our minds around the reality of it—and takes us having the faith to receive him!

"As many as received him, to them he gave the right to become children of God, even to those who believe in his name" (John 1:12). (Read John 3:1-8.)

"By grace you have been saved through faith; and that not of yourselves, it is the gift of God; not as a result of works that no one should boast" (Ephesians 2:8, 9).

Christ said, "Behold, I stand at the door and knock; if anyone hears my voice and opens the door, I will come in to him" (Revelation 3:20).

So, are you ready? Is there any need to wait, resist, or procrastinate any longer? Choosing Christ involves admitting to our sin, turning away from it, and asking Jesus to take control of our life. When we allow him to have control of our life, we are saying that we give him permission (yield, surrender) to use us for his glory. That moment is our hearts' conversion from death (the sin nature) to life in Christ (and eternal life with him today and for always). It's embracing him as Savior this side of death or meeting him as judge on the other side. It's alienation from God to a personal relationship *with* God. If you are ready to make that choice, read this prayer as an example of how you might communicate your willingness to trust him, and then pray sincerely, in your own words to God. He knows your heart and will honor your heartfelt words.

> Lord Jesus, I understand that you love me, and yet because of my sin, I am separated from you. I thank you for dying for my sins and know that you have given me eternal life with you. I trust you to have control of my life today and all the rest of my days. Help me to serve you and please you.

If that sincerely expresses your heart, and you have prayed similarly, God will fulfill all his promises and has done as he said he would.

"The witness is this, that God has given us eternal life, and this life is in his Son. He who has the Son has life; he who does not have the Son of God does not have life. These things I have written to you who believe in the name of the Son of God, in order that you may know that you have eternal life" (1 John 5:11-13).

Begin to thank God that he will never leave you (Hebrews 13:5). On the basis of God's Word (the Bible) you can know that Christ lives in you and that you have eternal life from the very moment you invite him in. When you have times of doubt, challenge, frustration, or sin—be sure to reach for the Bible to learn what God's truth is and begin applying what you have learned to your everyday life. Learning will involve trusting him with each detail of your life and as a result you will begin to experience the abundant life he has promised.

APPENDIX C
HOW TO GROW IN YOUR RELATIONSHIP WITH GOD

Studying God's Word in the context of a Bible-believing church where you can enjoy the fellowship ("the assembling of ourselves together," Hebrews 10:25) of like-minded believers in Jesus Christ will help you to learn to obey and follow God in your own life and then share God's Word with others.

Along with growing in your relationship with fellow believers and studying God's Word, there is growth through the Holy Spirit of God. God provided the Holy Spirit as our "helper." Jesus said in John 14:16–17, "And I will ask the Father, and he will give you another Helper, that he may be with you forever; that is the Spirit of truth, whom the world cannot receive, because it does not behold him or know him, but you know him because he abides with you, and will be in you." When you and I accepted Jesus as our Lord and Savior, the Holy Spirit came to abide (live) within us. Here are a few things that become ours the minute we put our trust in Christ, and the role the Holy Spirit plays in our new life:

- According to Romans 8:1–4, God gives us *new life* and teaches us not to "walk according to the flesh, but according to the Spirit." The Spirit is the power to walk according to God's ways and not our own flesh.

- Romans 8:5–8 assures us that the Holy Spirit *helps us* in our battle against sin, as long as we have asked the Lord into our life and he dwells within us. Additionally, James 1:14 says, "But each one is tempted when he is carried away and enticed by his own lust." We will be tempted, but we can ask the Holy Spirit to give us the *power* to conquer whatever temptations we experience.

- The Holy Spirit *leads us* as stated in Romans 8:14.

- We *become children of God* (Romans 8:15–16), and the Holy Spirit bears witness in our spirit that we are children of God.

- The Holy Spirit *helps us to pray.* (Romans 8:26–28)

- According to Galatians 5:22–25, " … the fruit of the Spirit is love, joy, peace, patience, kindness, goodness, faithfulness, gentleness, self-control; against such things there is no law. Those who belong to Christ Jesus have crucified the flesh with its passions and desires. If we live by the Spirit, let us also walk by the Spirit." When we belong to Christ, he gives us through the Holy Spirit, the ability to make new choices. We can leave our past sinful passions and desires and in exchange, choose to live according to God by living the fruitful and abundant life. To the degree that we can do that will depend upon our willingness to surrender to and follow God, and our maturity over the course of time.

- The Holy Spirit *resides in us* the moment we ask Jesus Christ into our life, but we can continually ask the Holy Spirit to *help us* in our walk with God. When we sin, we simply need to confess that sin, turn away from it with a desire not to continue in that sin, and ask the Holy Spirit to fill us. Ephesians 5:18 tells us as a command, "And do not get drunk with wine, for that is dissipation (a waste of time), but be filled with the Spirit..."

- John 7:37–39 shows us that the Holy Sprit is the source of a full and "overflowing" life.

Enjoy the adventure he has waiting for you!

APPENDIX D
THE ROCK STORY

Another Lesson in Life

A while back, I was reading about an expert on the subject of time management. One day this expert was speaking to a group of business students and, to drive home a point, used an illustration those students will never forget.

As this man stood in front of the group of high-powered overachievers he said, "Okay, time for a quiz." Then he pulled out a one-gallon, wide mouthed mason jar and set it on a table in front of him. Then he produced about a dozen fist-sized rocks and carefully placed them, one at a time, into the jar. When the jar was filled to the top and no more rocks would fit inside, he asked, "Is this jar full?" Everyone in the class said, "Yes."

Then he said, "Really?" He reached under the table and pulled out a bucket of gravel. He dumped some gravel in and shook the jar causing pieces of gravel to work themselves down into the spaces between the big rocks. Then he asked the group once more, "Is the jar full?"

By this time the class was onto him. "Probably not," one of them answered. "Good," he replied.

He reached under the table and brought out a bucket of sand. He started dumping the sand in and it went into all the spaces left between the rocks and the gravel. Once more he asked the question, "Is this jar full?" "No!" the class shouted. Once again he said, "Good!" Then he grabbed a pitcher of water and began to pour it in until the jar was filled to the brim. Then he looked up at the class and asked, "What is the point of this illustration?" One eager beaver raised his hand and said, "The point is, no matter how full your schedule is, if you try really hard, you can always fit some more things into it!"

"No," the speaker replied, "that's not the point. The truth this illustration teaches us is: If you don't put the big rocks in first, you'll never get them in at all."

What are the 'big rocks' in your life? A project that you want to accomplish? Time with your loved ones? Your faith, your education, your finances? A cause?

Teaching or mentoring others? Remember to put these *big rocks* in first or you'll never get them in at all.

So, tonight or in the morning when you are reflecting on this short story, ask yourself this question: What are the 'big rocks' in my life or business? Then, put those in your jar first.

Author Unknown

APPENDIX E
QUESTIONS TO HELP
BALANCE THE ACTIVE LIFE

The following are questions to ask yourself, your spouse and your children before starting, ending, changing employment, outside activities, ministry work, volunteering, etc.

Questions to Ask Yourself:

1. Have I completed other things I have been working on:

   - Sewing/Crafts
   - Cleaning
   - Inside my home/Outside my home
   - Other:

_____

_____

_____

2. Do I feel like this is something I would *love* to spend
    my time doing? Is it a passion?

    _____

3. Is this the right season of my life to do/start this?
    (Every season has its beauty.)

    _____

4. What is *most* important to me in my life? Does this
    blend with it?

    _____

5. What am I *living* for?

    _____

6. Am I *living* as though what is *most* important—*is*
    most important?

    _____

7. Will I use my spiritual gifts? Talents?

   _____

8. Is my home a haven that I have created for rest and relationship, or is it disorganized and chaotic?

   _____

9. Does the Holy Spirit fill me, empower me, and direct me?

   _____

Questions to Ask Yourself about You and Your Spouse:

1. Is my spouse in *complete* agreement? How do I know? Does my spouse think it's a "winner"?

   _____

2. Have we prayed about it together?

   _____

3. Will my spouse support me:
   - Emotionally (how....)
   - Physically (how....)
   - Encourage you (how....)
   - With time (how....)
   - Financially (how....)
   - Other:

   _____

4. Am I meeting my spouse's needs? Completely? Would my spouse answer as I have?

   _____

5. Is my spouse satisfied and fulfilled in our marriage?

   _____

6. Will this work/job/ministry/activity enhance or hinder our relationship together? Will this isolate us from each other or draw us closer together?

   _____

7. Does the Holy Spirit fill, empower, and direct our relationship?

_____

Questions to Ask Yourself about the Children (discuss with them):

1. Will I have more/less time with them?

_____

2. Can I still teach and train them like I want them to be taught and trained? Will I have the time?
   - Behavior
   - Manners
   - Chores
   - Responsibilities
   - School
   - Spiritually
   - Character
   - Other:

_____

3. What will my children say about this (job, ministry, activity, etc.) someday?

    _____

4. Will this job/activity isolate me from my children or draw me closer to them?

    _____

Questions to Consider Before Taking or Starting a Job :

1. Have I considered the financial start up costs? (Write it out on paper.)

    _____

2. Have I considered the risks to my finances, my family, my health, etc.?

    _____

3. How long will it be until I "break even" and start making/earning money?

    _____

4. Why do I want/need the income? Will I see it as income initially or will money continue to go back into the business or to paying childcare, etc.?

_____

5. How much do I need to clear each month to make monthly payments we have?

_____

6. How much time/attention will this require? Do I have those hours in the day?

_____

7. What will I trade/give up to do this job? (Consider who will clean, care for children, etc.)

_____

8. Do I have a written plan of application of goals, projected dates, etc.?

_____

9. What is my motivation, reason, pressure?

_____

10. Am I attempting to:
    - Meet a need in my life
    - Find fulfillment
    - Find significance
    - Help financially
    - Other:

    _____

11. Where is God in this? (Not "is he in this," but *where*—be specific.)

    _____

12. What am I communicating by doing this? (independence, supportive, rebellious, helpful, frustration, etc.) Is this what I want to communicate?

    _____

13. Have I *researched* the market? Or am I guessing?

    _____

14. Will this lead to any temptation? To greed? To lust? Other:

    _____

APPENDIX F
NUMBERING OUR DAYS

This article was published in the October 1, 1997 Alliance Life Magazine:

As a college student, I sat at my desk eating a dish of Jell-O listening to "Dueling Banjos." As the banjos "dueled" to high speed, so did the spoon to my mouth! Catching a glimpse of myself in the mirror, I chuckled. Realizing the music was influencing my actions, I turned off the radio to finish my dessert calmly.

Today, as the wife of a dentist/ministry leader, mother of three and seminar speaker, I still catch myself being influenced in ways that suggest things need to be "turned off" to get life back into perspective and balance.

It is amazing to see what some people do and what some refuse to do with the same twenty-four hours! We're told in Psalm 90:10: "The length of our days is seventy years—or eighty, if we have the strength" and verse 12 instructs us to "number our days aright, that we may gain a heart of wisdom" (NIV).

If I live to be seventy, I will have been given at least 25,550 days to live. I do not want to waste a moment. Nor do I want to be so busy that I can't enjoy the gifts God has given me in my family, friends, ministry, and life. I desire to live a balanced life and glorify the Lord in it.

In order to manage my time and maintain balance and order in my life, I ask myself these questions:

Is My Main Purpose in Life Being Fulfilled?

As believers our main purpose in life is to glorify God. That is why he created us (Isaiah 43:7; Psalm 86:12). This purpose gives me direction. How we initially do that depends on the different opportunities and situations God provides for us. Specific tasks and goals will need to be accomplished every day. Is what I'm doing being done for God's glory? Are the daily choices I am making being made in light of long-range goals and objectives?

How Is My Daily Quiet Time?

Did I pray to the Lord and read his Word to seek him today? What did I learn? Could I share it with someone else? This is my spiritual food. Would I miss a physical meal as easily as I might be tempted to miss time with God? If I haven't sought the Lord first (Matthew 6:33), why should I think my time would be balanced? Just as the Lord was able to multiply the fish and the loaves, I occasionally ask Him to multiply the time in my day. I'm often blessed to see the hands on the clock move more slowly. The Lord's time frame is different from our own (Psalm 90:4, 2 Peter 3:8).

Am I Being Realistic?

My list usually has 301 items to accomplish in a day! A reality check shows me that present needs, not perfection, are realistic. There must be time for each activity. Is time available? We all have different comfort levels. Is mine realistic for me? Will I be stressed? Is my health able to handle what I've been asked to do? Is this stage of life the right time to be doing certain things asked of me? Each age is a different season for our evaluation. Reevaluate and reset goals yearly, monthly, daily and even moment to moment if necessary to be best used of the Lord.

Am I Being Cautious?

"Yes" people need to ask this question. How long can a person keep adding to a schedule before the balance breaks? If I am adding something, what must I remove to keep life balanced? How will adding something affect my life, my family and other relationships? Do I *really* know what will be involved if I say yes? Learn to say "no" to what is good and "yes" to the best.

Instead of carrying my calendar, I carry a notebook. When asked to do something, a "blank" day looks like I'm automatically free. But if I have had several busy days or weeks, do I need that day for relief? I write the request in my notebook, pray about it, and get back with that person after I have had time to evaluate all of these questions.

Can I Be Flexible?

I was born an oak, not a willow, so the Lord has had to help me. In his sovereignty he gave us our son, Joey, who is multi-handicapped. I had no idea I could bend like I do at times! We need to be flexible to allow interruptions and changes to be truly effective for God. Many of his greatest blessings come when we least expect it. Are we flexible enough to drop everything if the Lord suddenly changes our direction? Are we willing to be flexible? It may take practice. Don't be easily discouraged.

Am I Delegating?

Delegating is difficult if you feel you need things done a certain way at a certain time. By delegating appropriately you are able to gain a few extra hours. "Dumping" what you don't want to be bothered with, however, is not the right way. That builds resentment in others.

Ask yourself: Is there someone who is better suited or better able to accomplish a part of this task? Is there someone who believes in what I'm doing who would lend a hand if I were to ask for help when things are overwhelming? Some people do not "do" simply because they are never asked. I have made it one of my goals to delegate appropriate chores to my children. We can do that in ministry as well.

Do I Have a Partner?

My husband and I work well together. We are thankful the Lord made us a team. At this moment he is helping to get a few things accomplished so I can write. I do the same for him when he is meeting a deadline.

You do not have to be married to have someone who will partner with you. Is there someone you really enjoy working with who would make a project more fun? Is there someone who encourages you to keep plugging away by praying for you? Equally as important, is there someone you can do that for as well? A partnership is giving and receiving. Good time managers are not just "takers" (Luke 6:38).

Am I Doing Things For the Right Reason?

If my motivation for doing something is to please or impress others, I will be stressed. Do I feel the need to do something because this person will think less of me if I don't do it? Am I doing it to be liked, popular or powerful?

A while back, our daughter Kristina was asked to join a third orchestra group. I told her I would commit the time to provide transportation and stay for rehearsal if she were willing to devote equal time to additional practice. I asked her to pray and seek the Lord. Her answer showed balance and brought relief: "Mom, I think I will only be trying to please the teacher, and I would miss the one day I get to play with Kathleen." The right reasons will lead to balance.

Am I Using My Spiritual Gift?

If you are using the gift God has blessed you with, you will in turn bless others and be energized as you use it. If you are using another's gift, you are likely to be frustrated and tired because it doesn't fit you. Are you loving where God has you serving, even when situations are difficult? Are you able to see the good that is happening as a result of how you use your gift? If you aren't sure what your gift is, begin to notice where you enjoy serving. Spiritual gift inventories can help determine your gifts.

Am I Taking Time to Rest, Exercise, Enjoy Life and Even Play?

We're really out of balance if we have forgotten what these things are! What do I enjoy that will refresh and allow me to complete the tasks God has given me? Is there someone I need to be accountable to? These times should not be looked upon as wasted time unless they are in excess and tilting the balance.

Are God's Priorities for Me Kept in Order?

"God is not a God of disorder but of peace" (1 Corinthians 14:33). When things aren't in order, it's usually because we've taken over. Lord, what should I do? Have I been sitting on the sidelines too long? Lord, where should I cut back if I've been in the game too long? If I like to play, is there a time limit I can put on some activities so that I can then get to work? If I'm too driven by projects, how long should I work at a task before taking a break and playing a game with the children, calling a friend to see how she is doing or kicking up my feet and reading a book? We need to be selective.

Am I Balanced?

Many people want a "formula" so they can feel good about what they are or are not doing. There is no set formula. You will know when you are out of balance. I know when I am! I get short with those I love most. I lose perspective. I get tired. But I am not perfect, so I continue to learn to live the balanced life by "turning off," "shutting down," "chilling out," and "cooling my jets."

We begin to feel the need for balance when problems with our feelings, emotions, attitudes and actions begin to spin out of control. If change is too long in coming, the stress and strain eventually will degrade our emotional, physical and spiritual health. My desire, like that of an athlete, is to better my time. I don't want to wait months or weeks to get things in balance. I want to correct the errors the moment I detect them so that I can run the race of life (1 Corinthians 9:24-27) with endurance and strength. Even marathon runners rest!

Ask the Lord to show you how to manage your time better. Ask him to give you balance as you make plans and establish goals. God will bless you as you seek his good and perfect will.

Appendix G
Year at a Glance

Goal and planning sheet for the year _____

My one main purpose in life is:

_____

Three specific goals that will help me to achieve my main purpose in life:

- _____
- _____
- _____

"There is an appointed time for everything. And there is a time for every event under heaven."
(Ecclesiastes 3:1)

	Personal Life	Spouse	Children	Business Work	Ministry Outreach	Leisure Relaxation	Financial Savings	Character Trait	Project
January									
February									
March									
April									
May									
June									
July									
August									
September									
October									
November									
December									

"And let the favor of the Lord our God be upon us: And do confirm for us the work of our hands; yes, confirm the work of our hands." (Psalm 90:17)

Hospitality Planner

OCCASION _____	Type Party
Date _____	Formal
Time _____	Informal
Theme _____	Casual
Colors _____	
Decorations _____	
	Size
	Intimate
MENU	Moderate
Hors D'oeuvres _____	Large
Appetizers _____	
Soup _____	
Salad _____	Service
Bread _____	Elegant
Main Course _____	Simple
Side Dish _____	Casual
Side Dish _____	
Side Dish _____	
Dessert _____	Things To Do
Coffee _____	
Beverages _____	One Week Prior
Additional Items Needed	_____
Chairs _____	_____
Tables _____	_____
Serving Dishes _____	
Other _____	Three Days Prior
Other _____	
Other _____	_____
	_____
Calls to Make	_____
Butcher _____	
Baker _____	Day Of Event
Grocer _____	_____
Caterer/Help _____	_____
Florist _____	_____

Guest List

Name	Phone	Check here if attending

Cindi Ferrini
CREATIVE MANAGEMENT FUNDAMENTALS
P.O. Box 360271
Cleveland, Ohio 44136
Phone and Fax 1.440.572.2019
www.cindiferrini.com